HISTORIC OSWESTRY

episodes from the past of a Welsh border town

by

JOHN PRYCE-JONES

Shropshire Libraries
1982

HISTORIC OSWESTRY is based on articles which were published in the Border Counties Advertizer between 1979 and 1981; the author is grateful to Mr. David Lewis, editor of the Advertizer, for permission to use these articles. Acknowledgement is also made for permission to reprint Holbache's Welsh ancestry (Leo Cooper), and the two Advertizer pages (British Library). Other illustrations in the text are from the local collections of Shropshire Libraries.

ISBN 0 903802 21 X

Cover design by Joyce Fogg.

Published by Shropshire Libraries, London Road, Shrewsbury.

Printed by Sayce Brothers, Llandrindod Wells.

Pryce-Jones, John
  Historic Oswestry
  1. Oswestry (Shropshire)—History
  I. Title
  942.24'51   DA690.08

ISBN 0-903802-21-X

Contents

Oswestry is the liberal, the best endowed of cities;
The beloved of heaven that draws me to it.
Oswestry the strong fort of conquerors; the London of Powis;
Where the houses are well stored with wine and the land is rich.
Its school is celebrated, and its city for preachers and men of science.
God is present in its beautiful temple—
A church adorned with rich challices,
And with bells and a rich toned organ.
No better choir is there from it to Canterbury:
None in which there is correcter singing,
Or the habiliments more suitable.
To White Minster I know no convent superior.
The handsomest and best drest women are those of Oswestry.
It resembles Cheapside in merchandise.
And its people are honest and unanimous.
God's grace be with the city, and those that dwell therein;
May God be its guardian and kind preserver.

Guto'r Glyn (d. 1493)
(translated into English)

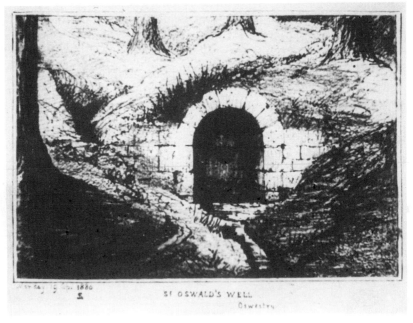

St. Oswald's Well

4

Introduction

Described quite accurately as a small market town on the Welsh border, Oswestry must appear, to the casual visitor, as a sleepy place, where little of any consequence ever happens, or has ever happened. Nestling in the foothills of Wales above the Shropshire plain, the town lies just off the Holyhead trunk road, close to but no longer part of the rail network; it lacks any major waterway, and has suffered a near-ruinous sequence of setbacks in the past twenty years. Ifton colliery, the railway works, and Park Hall army camp have all closed down, and the Oswestry area was at the centre of the disastrous foot and mouth epidemic in the late 1960s. With regard to tourism, Oswestry and the surrounding countryside have frequently been passed over by guide books, possibly as a result of the area's geographical and cultural situation: often described as a Welsh town in England, Oswestry nevertheless is not a part of modern Wales, yet sits somewhat awkwardly on the northern borders of Shropshire. Despite all these disadvantages and obstacles in the way of success, modern Oswestry shows the same sort of resilience and self-sufficiency which it has exhibited throughout its life; by developing the town's age-old market role, capitalising on the district's undoubted tourist potential, and encouraging new industry to the area, the town now shows a more prosperous face than it has for many a year.

In the different chapters of this booklet I hope to illustrate elements of continuity in Oswestry's development from its foundation by the Normans to the present day. Misfortune has often beset the town-it has endured many disastrous fires, both accidentally-started and in warfare; it has been ravaged by both Welsh and English troops; it has suffered deadly outbreaks of plague. A twenty-five year period in the 17th century saw the loss of the staple trade of the town—wool—to Shrewsbury, and the destruction of the castle. On several occasions Oswestry has had to adapt quickly to changed circumstances, or face ruinous decline.

Oswestry's story, much of it unfortunately obscured or forgotten, is one of long-term resilience and independence of spirit. It is a story punctuated by strange events and incidents of national importance—the foundation of Oswestry School 575 years ago, the time when Oswestry took on the might of English soccer almost single-handed, or the reverberations generated by the Liberals' by-election victory in 1904. The town has reared many famous people, such as Edward Lhuyd, Thomas Bray, Wilfred Owen, David Holbache and Sir Henry Walford Davies, all men of culture. Today Oswestry seethes with life, be it in the many churches and chapels, the inns and hotels, the many local societies, or out on the sports fields. Oswestry is a busy place, a town with a character and atmosphere all its own.

A Turbulent Past

dates of importance in Oswestry's history

641   King Penda of Mercia defeats King Oswald of Northumbria at Maserfelth.

1086   Domesday Book. Oswestry is not mentioned by name, but sheriff Rainald is recorded as having built a castle, called L'oeuvre, in the hundred of Mersete, almost certainly Oswestry Castle.

1149–1157   Lordship of Oswestry is held by Madog ap Maredudd of Powys. Oswestry Castle rebuilt.

1188   William Fitzalan, Earl of Arundel, gives a sumptuous banquet in Oswestry Castle in honour of Baldwin, Archbishop of Canterbury, and Giraldus Cambrensis.

1189–1190   'Y Siarter Gwtta'. William Fitzalan grants Oswestry its first charter. The Lord receives into his protection the burgesses of 'Blancminster' (another name for Oswestry) and grants them the same liberties as Shrewsbury, an act intended to strengthen Oswestry as a market town.

1211   King John sets out from Oswestry against Llywelyn ap Iorwerth.

1215   King John burns Oswestry to the ground—John Fitzalan had turned against him.

1228   Fair of four days' duration granted to the town.

1233   Llywelyn ap Iorwerth burns Oswestry to the ground.

1263   Oswestry's second charter—the burgesses are given the right to make by-laws for the profit and improvement of the borough.

1277   Edward I initiates the building of the town walls.

1324   Edmund Fitzalan grants two shops in Leg Street to the burgesses.

1397   Richard Fitzalan, Earl of Arundel, attainted and executed, and his lands granted by King Richard II to the Earl of Wiltshire.

1399   First Royal charter, subsequent to Richard II adjourning Parliament from Shrewsbury to Oswestry in 1398.

1400   Owain Glyndwr's followers burn Oswestry to the ground.

1403   Glyndwr uses Oswestry as his base prior to the battle of Shrewsbury.

1407   Traditionally the foundation date for Oswestry School, though 1404 seems equally likely. Thomas Fitzalan's charter forbids his rural subjects from selling their wares elsewhere unless they are first offered for sale at Oswestry market.

1536   Act of Union of Wales with England places Oswestry on the English side of the border.

1530s	John Leland, historian and traveller, visits Oswestry at the end of the decade.
1542	Fire destroys much of Oswestry.
1544	Oswestry burned again.
1559	Outbreak of plague—"the sweating sickness"—forces the movement of the market to the Croeswylan area on the town outskirts.
1567	Yet another disastrous fire in Oswestry.
1585	Another outbreak of plague forces the market's removal to Knockin.
1604	Inscription date on Llwyd Mansion, built by John Lloyd of Llanforda.
1616	James I grants Oswestry a charter, confirming a previous Order made by Elizabeth I.
1621	Welsh wool trade, Oswestry's chief source of wealth, thrown open by Royal Proclamation.
1644	Oswestry falls to Parliamentary forces led by the Earl of Denbigh and Colonel Thomas Mytton. The Civil War results in the demolition of Oswestry Castle.
1660	Edward Lloyd of Llanforda builds the Coach and Dogs as an inn. Birth of Edward Lhuyd.
1673	Charles II's charter to Oswestry.
1709	Death of Edward Lhuyd.
1771	The Black Gate is pulled down.
1776	Oswestry School removes from Church Terrace to Cae'r Groes, the lands granted by the Williams-Wynn family.
1781	Old grammar school buildings used as the town's workhouse.
1782	New Gate, Beatrice Gate, and Willow Gate are demolished.
1791	Opening of the House of Industry at Morda.
1808	London to Holyhead mail-coaches begin running through Oswestry.
1845	Shrewsbury, Oswestry and Chester Junction Railway authorised.
1848	Oswestry Markets and Fairs Bill enacted. Shrewsbury and Chester Railway's line between Oswestry and Gobowen opens on December 23rd.
1849	First issue of Oswestry Advertiser and Railway Guide published in January. Powis Hall and Cross Markets open on June 6th. July 4th brings the opening of the cattle and horse markets.
1864	Cambrian Railways formed by the amalgamation of the Llanidloes & Newtown, Oswestry & Newtown, Oswestry, Ellesmere & Whitchurch, and Newtown & Machynlleth Railway Companies. The Aberystwyth & Welsh Coast Railway joins a year later.
1879	Oswestry Football Club provides nine of the Welsh XI which

	plays England at Kennington.
1891	Closure of the New Trefonen Colliery, the last pit worked in the Oswestry coalfield.
1893	Birth of Wilfred Owen at Plas Wilmot, Weston Lane.
1904	Liberal by-election victory.
1918	Park Hall is destroyed by fire. The Hall and its grounds had been utilised by the army from early in the First World War.
1921	Formal opening of the Robert Jones & Agnes Hunt Orthopaedic Hospital at Gobowen.
1966	Closure of the Oswestry to Gobowen rail link in November.
1967	Start of the disastrous foot and mouth epidemic at Nantmawr in October.
1968	End of foot and mouth epidemic in June. Closure of Ifton Colliery, the last in North Shropshire.

An unknown artist's impression of Oswestry Castle

Outpost and Gateway

the early history of Oswestry

The town of Oswestry was a Norman foundation: Domesday Book, produced in 1086, does not mention Oswestry at all, though it does record a castle, L'oeuvre, built by Rainald, sheriff of Shropshire, in the Hundred of Mersete near to the township of Meresberie, present-day Maesbury. There is no record of the name 'Oswestry' before 1272, though the Welsh 'Croes Oswallt' appears in 1254. Prior to this date the town was known as Blancminster or Album Monasterium, presumably in reference to its whitish parish church. Domesday Book shows how the Welsh-sounding 'Maesbury' derives from the Old English 'Maeresburg', signifying a fortified place on the boundary; the name 'Mersete' is similarly 'Maersaete'-the dwellers on the boundary. Thus the Oswestry area in 1086 was under English rule, and it is likely that it had been so for many years, since the boundary referred to is of course Offa's Dyke and its contemporary, Wat's Dyke. The Normans included Mersete in Shropshire, acknowledging the area as a part of England, and the Hundred's townships possessed English names, such as Weston, Halston, Melverley, Woolston and Whittington. The tenants too bore English names like Edric, Seward, and Edwin. This was understandable, since the Oswestry area had long been a part of the Kingdom of Mercia—certainly by the late 8th century when the dyke was constructed. Possibly the connection goes back even further, if Maserfelth, the battle where Penda of Mercia defeated Oswald of Northumbria, really is Oswestry. If so, the area was likely to have been under Mercian influence by the mid 7th century.

However, though it is true that Oswestry was English at this time, the area was very much an outpost. It is significant that Meresberie needed fortification: Domesday Book refers to the wasted lands in the district, probably ravaged by Alfgar and Gruffydd ap Llywelyn in their fight against Edward the Confessor. The dyke, the Norman castle, and the name 'Mersete' all acknowledge some sort of frontier status. The evidence of Domesday Book shows that the hills to the west of Maesbury were inhabited by Welshmen; when Oswestry's western townships emerge, they all bear Welsh names such as Trefarclawdd, Cynynion, Bryn and Treflach, and Domesday Book lists the tenant of Brogyntyn as 'Madoc', possibly a son of Bleddyn ap Cynfyn, Prince of Powys. Furthermore, fifty-three Welshmen are recorded among the Hundred's sub-tenants—fifty-three out of the total of sixty-seven for the whole of Shropshire. Clearly Oswestry was not exclusively English.

Immediately after the Conquest, the Hundred of Mersete was among the lands granted by King William to Earl Roger of Montgomery. He in turn granted it to Warine, sheriff of Shropshire, and from him it passed to Rainald, the tenant in 1086. Rainald was followed by Alan FitzFlaad, whose descendants, the Fitzalans, ruled Oswestry for the next 475 years as Lords of

11

Oswestry, and subsequently as Earls of Arundel. In the 12th century, the family held the position of sheriff of Shropshire as if by right, and thus they were able to keep their Lordships of Clun and Oswestry outside the jurisdiction of the shire, running them independently as 'petty kings', a situation accepted by the Crown and perpetuated in return for a secure Welsh border. The Fitzalans ruled Oswestry well, developing it from its original function of a garrison and outpost of Norman rule, into a flourishing market town.

For many years unrest was an accepted part of life on the Welsh border. Initially the Fitzalans' hold on the town and its castle was far from secure, largely as a consequence of external events: the civil war between King Stephen and the Empress Matilda. William Fitzalan I sided with Matilda, rebelled against the King, and in 1138 was forced to abandon his territories. Whilst England was preoccupied with internal strife, the Welsh princes took advantage of the situation to recover previous losses, so that between 1149 and 1157 Madog ap Maredudd, Prince of Powys, ruled over the Lordship of Oswestry. Whilst in occupation he extended, or possibly rebuilt, Oswestry castle, but with the accession of Henry II, Matilda's son, William Fitzalan returned to favour and his lands, but not to peace. For both the Fitzalans and Oswestry the years of the Plantagenets were troubled times which saw the town sacked and burnt on several occasions, and which witnessed conflict both between Welsh and English, and between the King and his barons.

In 1165 Henry II set out from Oswestry against Owain Gwynedd, in what proved to be a highly unsuccessful campaign, cut short by stormy weather and Welsh resistance. In 1211 Oswestry was the base from which King John marched against Llywelyn Fawr and North Wales, and in 1215 John returned to the town, this time in his struggle with the barons, and burnt it to the ground. Llywelyn visited the town in 1233, and he too burnt it down. Understandably, the town was walled in the 1270s on the orders of Edward I.

Paradoxically, it was at the time of these misfortunes that the foundations were being laid which broadened Oswestry's base, and developed its potential as a market town. William Fitzalan III granted the town its first charter, the 'Siarter Gwtta' or short charter, in 1189-1190, receiving into his protection the burgesses of Blancminster and granting them the same customs and liberties as those of Shrewsbury, a move calculated to strengthen Oswestry's market. In 1228 a fair of four days' duration was allowed—a privilege which upset neighbouring rival boroughs, but which was confirmed in 1263 by the town's second charter, which also allowed the burgesses to make by-laws for the profit and improvement of the borough. Edmund Fitzalan added to the burgesses' privileges in 1324, and Oswestry's growing prosperity was further consolidated in 1399 when Richard II granted the town its first Royal charter, and in 1407, with Thomas Fitzalan's charter. By the start of the 15th century the character of Oswestry had changed quite dramatically.

In 1276, Llywelyn ap Gruffydd, ordered by the English to pay homage to Edward I in London, refused to do so, but offered instead to meet the King in either Oswestry or Montgomery. Oswestry was at this time in the midst of the construction work on the town walls, yet subtly the town was beginning to change: the twin roles of 'outpost' and 'gateway' were being merged, and the town was becoming less an English stronghold, more neutral territory. This change took a long time, and Oswestry was to witness scenes of fire and carnage 120 years after Llywelyn's death. Nevertheless, the new role was ideally suited to Oswestry, reflecting as it did the town's geographical and linguistic position. Over the years the division between the area's English town and lowland and the Welsh hill country had grown less clear cut. By the early 15th century several Welshmen were burgesses of the town, and Welshmen were buying and selling property there. Oswestry School's founder, David Holbache, and his wife Gwenhwyfar both had Welsh pedigrees, and the list of the School's first trustees included such names as Evan ap Atha ap Evan, David ap Thomas, and Cadwaller ap Evan. Oswestry was still seen as a legitimate target for the followers of Owain Glyndwr in 1400, but the trend was towards integration and compromise, and saw the re-establishment of the area's Welsh character. The post-Edwardian peace and the development of Oswestry's trading role accelerated the process, whose results can be seen in the 16th and 17th century parish registers, which contain many examples of the Welsh form of nomenclature. Local field and place names are overwhelmingly Welsh, and in the 1530s the historian John Leland noted Welsh equivalents of Oswestry's English street names: for instance Stryd y Llan for Church Street. Oswestry was also a centre of Welsh culture in the 15th and 16th centuries, attracting well-known bards such as Guto'r Glyn, Gutun Owain and Tudur Aled. Intertwined with all this was the Welsh wool trade. The great weekly market held in the town can be seen both as the fruition of the process of integration and as the lynch-pin which held the fabric of Oswestry together; the continuance of the market was essential to the maintenance of the status quo. Though the town of Oswestry by Tudor times had become "as Welsh as any town in Wales", the situation changed once more with the succession of the Stuarts. The loss of the woollen staple in 1621 was the watershed—henceforth Oswestry would become English again.

Already the Act of Union of England and Wales, passed in 1536 under Henry VIII, had placed the Lordship of Oswestry firmly in Shropshire. The trend towards reform of the Welsh border initiated with the establishment of the Council of the Marches of Wales was confirmed. Certainly the national boundary was drawn "without reference to racial, historical or geographical considerations"; nevertheless by the Act Oswestry became an integral part of England. The loss of the staple, and the resultant economic decline, accentuated the process of anglicization—Oswestry's market became more a local affair, depriving the town of 'new blood' from Wales. Again, change took time of course and Richard Gough of Myddle, writing of Oswestry in the 1680s, could still speak of the "Welshmen" of the town, but stagnation and the area's reduced importance made Oswestry by Napoleonic times an

English town. In 1795 the Vicar of St. Oswald's informed the Bishop of St. Asaph that the people desired more English, and in 1814 Welsh services in the parish church were discontinued altogether. That the economic factor was crucial can be seen from the way that this decline was arrested in the mid 19th century; the period of growth symbolised by the opening of the new markets in 1849, and by the success of the Cambrian Railways, was responsible for today's cultural balance, with four Welsh chapels in Oswestry indicative of a flourishing Welsh community.

A Visitation of the Plague

It was in the 16th century that Oswestry reached the height of its prosperity, and Elizabeth I's reign was a period of growth matched only by the burst of economic activity in the mid 19th century. The Welsh woollens industry was at the root of this 'boom', Oswestry having the good fortune to acquire a virtual monopoly of the trade. It is strange then that this period was also one of grave misfortune for the town. There were disastrous fires in 1542, 1544 and 1567, and in 1559 there was a visitation by the plague — an occurrence commemorated to this day by the Croeswylan Stone, and by the naming of Croeswylan School. It speaks volumes for Oswestry's resilience that the town survived these fires, this epidemic and a smaller outbreak in 1585, especially since the plague of 1559 was from all accounts an attack of great force. William Cathrall, in his 'History of Oswestry' claimed that the disease "consigned to the grave, within one year, more than five hundred of the inhabitants". The dead-cart, the bell, and the cry of "bring out your dead" all must have been part of the story. Isaac Watkin described the symptoms of the disease, known as the 'sweating sickness', in the following terms—"the invasion of the disease was generally quite sudden, some persons experiencing a sensation as of a hot vapour extending over the body, while others felt as if consumed by an internal fire. There was violent fever, pain in the head and limbs, prostration of strength, hurried breathing, great thirst, delirium and excessive restlessness. Shortly after, . . . a profuse clammy fetid perspiration broke out over the whole body, the thirst became more intolerable, and the patients either died in a state of delirium or coma, or recovered as suddenly as they had been first attacked". Certainly, if this is a true picture, it must have been a horrifying experience, with the sole comfort being that "all danger was considered to be at an end if the patient survived the first twenty-four hours".

Luckily, the parish register for 1559 survives, and it includes margin notes made at the time of the plague by John Price, then Vicar of St. Oswald's. He kept a personal record of the daily toll of the disease among his parishioners between July 11th 1559 and January 12th 1560. Deaths recorded rose from twenty in the month of April 1559 to a peak of one hundred and thirty-seven for September of the same year, falling gradually back until the plague passed over in January 1560. The figures are quite staggering. Three hundred and seventy-two parishioners died in the four key months from August to November, and four hundred and fifty-four in the second half of the calendar year, at a time when the normal rate was between two hundred and two hundred and fifty.

Burials recorded, St Oswald's Parish Church, Oswestry :

April 1559	20	September	137
May	25	October	119
June	27	November	52
July	48	December	34
August	64	January 1560	15

Behind these bare figures many personal tragedies are concealed. Whole families were struck down at once, perhaps an inevitable consequence of the cramped living conditions and basic sanitary arrangements of the time. Thus we have "Katharinge Baker, Anne vz. Thomas, M'gret vz. Thomas & Jane vz. Thomas buried the xviij day" of June, and on July 11th, "John ap David, Agnes vz. David, & Alice vz. David buried the same daye". Incidentally, it is interesting to note the prevalence of Welsh surnames in supposedly English Oswestry.

In 1559 Oswestry was, in fact, still very much a traditional Welsh border town, retaining clear signs of its troubled Marcher past, such as its walls and fortified gates. The years of the Tudors and their predecessors of the House of York were times of transition to a recognisably modern world, but at the time of the plague, Ludlow Castle was still the headquarters for the Council of the Marches of Wales, and it was a mere 150 years since Oswestry had been burnt down by the followers of Owain Glyndwr. However Oswestry was then, as now, predominantly a market town, living from its roots with Wales. The traveller John Leland could write in the late 1530s of Oswestry's " tymbre and slatid" houses, its three main streets within the walls, Bailey, Cross and New Gate Streets—and its suburbs outside each gate, and he could solidly state that "the towne standith most by sale of cloth made in Wales".

It is in this light—of a town based firmly on trade, relying on market tolls, its inns and shops dependent on the market-day custom—that the plague of 1559 should be considered. Understandably the Welsh weavers and the groups of drapers and merchants were unwilling to enter a plague-ridden town, with the result that the market was moved beyond the town walls to the present-day Croeswylan area, then well into the country. Thus the people of Oswestry suffered in two ways. They were in danger of their lives, and they also suffered financially: stall holders, innkeepers, and the toll-collectors at the four gates all lost money through the plague, even if they survived the disease.

In addition to the parish register, another account of the plague's effects has survived. This is the "Accompt of Richard ap Lley, Muringer of the town of Oswestry, for and from the xvj day of September in the second yere of our sovraynge Lady Elizabeth". This account shows graphically the extent to which Oswestry's trade and livelihood was hit, describing how traders were struck down with the pestilence, took to flight to avoid it or, if they stayed and survived, lost their customers. The Muringer begins by stating that the "accomtante doth asc alowaunce for rent bayted to the Towlers (tolltakers) for one quarter in considracion of the Plage . . .", and he then continues by outlining the plight of each group of traders or manufacturers in the town. In the case of the glovers "the sayde acomptaunt dothe asc alowaunce for them that are deade or fled, and them that are in decaye; and fyrst, Thomas ap John Wyling, being a poore man (five others fled, etc)". The fate of the ale-sellers was no better: "Edward Lloyd praythe alowaunce for a quarter, 12d; David Glover the elder, in lycke manner 14d; Richard Salter was long sycke, and praythe alowance 14d; Thomas Glover praythe alowaunce for half a yere, aledginge that he sold no alle for that space 20d". An irreverent observer might note that, if Thomas Glover spoke the truth and did sell no ale, then Oswestry must have been in a sorry state!

Today Oswestry remembers this episode in its history through the Croeswylan Stone. This stone's history has been disputed, though its connection with the plague in some form is not argued. Isaac Watkin wrote simply that the stone "formed the base of a cross erected in the vicinity", set where the market moved to during the epidemic. It is possible that the base was all that remained in 1559, and that the market traders washed their money in the water which collected in the hollow. Watkin mentioned that, in more recent times, "it was customary for the country people to wash their money in the water stored in the cavity" of the cross base. However, this suggestion goes against the evidence of the name 'croeswylan', which translates as the 'cross of weeping', which implies that the cross was erected in 1559, or at least was standing in that year.

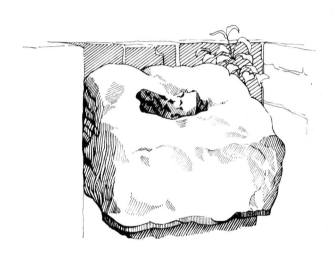

The Croeswylan Stone

A Market for Wool

Welsh woollens in the 16th and 17th centuries

"The towne standith most by sale of cloth made in Wales". (Leland).
"Tis a place of good traffick, for Welsh-Cottons especially,which are of a very fine, thin, or (if you will) slight texture;of which great quantities are weekly vended here". (Camden).

There is little in Oswestry today to remind us of one major aspect in the town's history: Welsh woollens. To men such as John Leland and William Camden, the wool trade was Oswestry's main source of income and employment. For instance, in 1619, the Shrewsbury Drapers' Company reputedly did £2,000 worth of business in woollens at Oswestry's market every week. Such trade has left an obvious mark on the streets of Shrewsbury—the splendid half-timbered mansions which give the town centre its character—but Oswestry has few reminders of the important position it once held in the Welsh woollens industry. The Woolpack Inn closed several years ago, and is now incorporated into a garage in Willow Street. Oswestry never had a particularly well organised market for woollens—there was no 'cloth hall'—and the railway boom of the mid to late nineteenth century has left the town with a predominantly Victorian appearance. Surnames found locally provide some sort of clue—Glovers and Weavers, and Walkers, Banners and Tuckers (these three names deriving from the fulling process) indicate some kind of woollens industry in our past.

The woollen trade was always a labour-intensive business, with a long chain of processes and specialised crafts; the wool went through many changes before it produced fabrics and clothing. It was first cleaned, sorted and carded, then spun. Next it was woven into a cloth by a weaver, using the traditional warp-and-weft technique, then passed on to the fuller who, at the fulling mill, thickened the nap of the cloth. The cloth was stretched or tentered to give it shape, teased or cottoned to raise the nap, sheared to make it smooth, and finally dyed. This chain was geographical too. Much of Wales was then, as now, moorland pasture suitable for little else but sheep grazing. The scattered farmsteads provided the labour for the initial processes, and the lower reaches of many streams proved ideal for working fulling mills. However, Wales's geography, and the lack of capital for investment within Wales meant that the trade remained a subsistence living. The markets were spread along the Welsh border and beyond, and capital was available here, a fact which was the key to the trade's prosperity. Most of all, direction came from the powerful Shrewsbury drapers. T. C. Mendenhall, in his study of the trade, 'The Shrewsbury drapers and the Welsh wool trade in the 16th and 17th centuries', comments that "Welsh cloth . . . was incapable of preventing the larger share of the profits going to a foreign element in the trade—the Border drapers who marketed the cloth for export". Welsh cloth was often not finished until it reached Shrewsbury, and even Shropshire was only a stopping-off point for the goods. What began as wool in North Wales was characteristically sold by the weaver at Oswestry to the draper from Shrewsbury, transported south to London by pack-horse, and sold for export at Blackwell Hall in the City of London, finally arriving at Rouen in France.

Oswestry was perhaps fortunate in gaining its place in this chain. However, once in possession of its 'rights', the town hung on to them tenaciously, though dogged by a succession of misfortunes. The Welsh cloth industry had originally grown up in south Wales, but gradually moved north, partly through the desire to move clear of the officially controlled towns of the south. By 1326 Shrewsbury, like Cardiff and Carmarthen, was a 'staple town'—the right to purchase the wool was vested with a body of the town's merchants. The trade grew, partly through exemption from trading standards, partly through the success of the Border markets. By the reign of Edward I Oswestry had become a meeting place for the Welsh weavers and clothiers and the English drapers, and the town increased in importance partly through historical chance and partly through geographical location. Rivalled by Chester, Welshpool, Wrexham, and, of course, Shrewsbury, Oswestry in the sixteenth century was the successful bidder for the market. Mendenhall wrote that "situated in the foothills where the rugged Berwyn mountains of North Wales slope off in gentle valleys to join the broad Severn plain, Oswestry was at once the last outpost of England and the entrance to Wales". As so often in Oswestry's past, the town's location proved of major significance. The weavers could go to the market and return home in a day, and the Shrewsbury merchants did not have too far to travel either, though their journey was endangered by highwaymen. Oswestry was, in effect, neutral ground and its choice a compromise. This was all well and good for a time but, seen objectively, Oswestry had no real advantage of its own.

What was Oswestry like at this time? Certainly it must have been a busy place, with such large sums of money changing hands within the town walls every week. In addition to the Welsh wool, some English wool was also brought to the market, draped into cloth, and sold for the London markets. The market took place on Mondays, and was "a simple affair". There were also three major fairs—in May, August, and November. Trading was not open to all but was limited to the drapers of Oswestry, Shrewsbury, Whitchurch and Coventry. Of these groups, the Shrewsbury Drapers' Company was by far the largest. Towards the end of Oswestry's reign as chief market, the status quo was affected by 'interlopers' who legally should not have been trading there—shearmen from Shrewsbury trying to invade the drapers' territory, and, more significantly, London merchants seeking to exclude the Border drapers from the business altogether. It would have been a cramped state of affairs, with trade being carried on in certain houses "anciently reserved for the market" since no special building housed the cloth market. Oswestry still had its walls and its castle; its houses would have been mainly half-timbered, tightly packed and overhanging. Many would have been newly built, since there had been disastrous fires in 1542, 1544, and 1567. Presumably, such a large influx of traders each week would have attracted other businesses to serve the market. Furthermore, the trade must have filled the civic coffers, as there was a toll of 2d on every cloth going in or out of Oswestry, and approximately £3 was raised each week in this way. Obviously wool was very important to Oswestry's prosperity.

It has been noted that Oswestry won the monopoly of the Welsh wool trade largely through being in the right place at the right time, rather than through any great merit or advantage within the town itself. For the moment, the compromise suited Oswestry, but the town in the long term was in an unavoidably weak position. Despite having the market itself, and some local involvement in the woollens industry, Oswestry lacked influence due to its size and lack of wealth. The most powerful participant in the trade remained the Shrewsbury Drapers' Company, who in 1602 were doing half the total trade at the market. Shrewsbury was much more powerful than Oswestry in every respect. It had been a free incorporated town since the 12th century, and had returned Members of Parliament since the 13th century; as an indication of relative wealth, Shrewsbury's ship money assessment in 1635 was £420, whilst Oswestry's was only £21. The local drapers were poorly organised in comparison with their Shrewsbury counterparts; the latter had formed themselves into a separate company in 1461, and had gained a tight hold over the trade, whilst the Oswestry drapers remained in one company with the mercers. Oswestry's lack of direction is evident in the controversy which took place between 1619 and 1623 over the control of the trade—the only two petitions received by the Privy Council from Oswestry were sent in conjunction with Shrewsbury. Similarly, when in 1582 Chester sought to take over the monopoly, Shrewsbury's protest to the Council mentions Oswestry seemingly as an afterthought : ". . . whatsoever is before-said for Shrewsbury towching the injurye sought toward them, and their perill, is also to be said . . for Owcestrie, and thus much also more, that Owcestrie . . . hath no suche other benefites and meanes of helpe as we have, but dependeth wholie upon their market of buyeng of such Clothes, and the making and workmanship thereof, so as if the said Staple should proceade (i.e. to Chester) they were to be utterlie undon". Though Shrewsbury came to Oswestry's aid on this occasion, it would be scarcely reassuring to Oswestrians to realise how well Shrewsbury knew their predicament.

Oswestry was unfortunate in that, at the very time the town gained its monopoly and needed good fortune to keep hold of it, it was beset by a series of unforseeable events which could only have served to undermine its strength and confidence. Apart from the three major fires, there were outbreaks of the plague in both 1559 and 1585. In the sphere of local government, uncertainty prevailed at a time when stability was required. The Fitzalans, who had controlled the Lordship since the early twelfth century, had recently been succeeded by the Howards, who had gained the Earldom of Arundel, and thus the Barony of Oswestry, by marriage. However, the Howards were (and still are) a Roman Catholic family, and in Elizabethan England, especially just after the Armada, this was not conducive to royal favour. Philip Howard, created Earl of Arundel in 1580, was attainted as a traitor in 1590. The Lordship of Oswestry passed to the Crown, and remained in royal hands until 1603, when James I granted it to Thomas Howard, Earl of Suffolk and Philip's half-brother. A survey of the area made for Suffolk by John Norden shows how standards had fallen under royal control. It was also a time when Oswestry's burgesses were fighting, with both justification and success, for reforms in Oswestry's local government, and asserting their rights against those of their Lord but, despite this, it is clear that when local matters reached London in search of a decision, the support and interest of men of influence at court was vital. In 1582, for example, it is thought that Chester's case fell only because of the intervention of the Lord Chancellor, Sir Thomas Bromley, a Shropshire man. However, for much of the crucial period, that sort of influence was lacking for Oswestry.

Oswestry's monopoly was in a vulnerable position at the start of the 17th century, in spite of the support of James I's favourite, his Lord Chamberlain Thomas Howard. Both Elizabeth I and James I had granted out licences, charters, and monopolies in various spheres of the economy, seeing in them a useful source of revenue for the Treasury, but Parliament increasingly viewed this policy as a restriction on trade, an attack on 'ancient liberties', and an example of royal abuse of its prerogatives. This reaction caused James problems throughout his reign and led, in 1624, to Parliament passing the Statute of Monopolies which sought to prevent the practice. Clearly the monopolistic tendencies in the Welsh wool trade would be seen unfavourably in this light.

Arguably, Oswestry's hold over the market could only remain intact so long as the situation stayed calm and nothing controversial occurred which would attract Parliament's attention. Unfortunately this was impossible. In many ways it was a time of unrest and upheaval. There was a recession in the wool trade at large, brought about by a combination of domestic and continental factors. The Shrewsbury drapers' role as middlemen was steadily being pressed by both the London wool merchants—capitalising on the feeling for free trade and looking for more personal profit—and by the Welsh weavers, who were realising what a barrier the Drapers' Company was to their greater prosperity. Finally, rivalry between Oswestry and Shrewsbury appears to have increased at this time.

The Shrewsbury drapers would without doubt have preferred the market to have been held in Shrewsbury, saving them a weekly journey to Oswestry. They resented the tolls imposed by Oswestry, and, from contemporary accounts, they scarcely enjoyed their excursion to and from the market, as the road was beset with highwaymen. In 1583 the Drapers' Company minutes include the entry, "Ordered, that no Draper set out for Oswestry on Mondays before six o'clock, on forfeiture of six shillings and eightpence; and that they wear their weapons all the way, and go in company—not to go over the Welsh Bridge before the bell toll six." Oswestry viewed every action of Shrewsbury and its drapers with suspicion

—understandably, given the relative strength of the two towns; in 1582 a clause was inserted in Oswestry's new articles forbidding Shrewsbury men from gaining burghal status unless they were resident in Oswestry. In 1609 the Earl of Suffolk accused the Drapers' Company of plotting to remove the staple to Shrewsbury. The Company denied this, but in reply complained of Oswestry's tolls, of interlopers at the market, and of lack of co-operation from Oswestry over the standard of cloth. In the matter of the monopoly, Oswestry needed the friendship of Shrewsbury far more than the county town required Oswestry's goodwill, but little effort apparently was made in Oswestry to cultivate any sort of alliance at this time.

Oswestry's position as Border staple is possibly the most influential and prestigious status that the town has ever reached. In 1582 the rejection of Chester's petition had confirmed Oswestry's rights, and as late as 1614 the town's privileges were enumerated by the Privy Council: discussing the activities of a London merchant who had done business with the weavers of Machynlleth, the Council made clear, in an Order of February 1614, that Welsh cloth could only be exported through Oswestry, that all Border drapers could trade at Oswestry, but that London merchants had to stay at home and buy their cloth at Blackwell Hall. However, this clarification was not wholly beneficial. Oswestry market, and the Shrewsbury drapers' hold over it, looked more and more like a monopoly, ripe for reform.

Therefore, when James I's third Parliament assembled, in January 1621, business included a "Bill of Welsh Cottons", or, to give it its full title, a "Bill for the Free Trade and Traffic of Welsh Cloths, Cottons, Friezes, Linings and Plains, in and through the Kingdom of England and the Dominion of Wales". The situation had worsened considerably for Oswestry since 1614. Thomas Howard had fallen from favour, found guilty of embezzlement in his capacity as Lord Treasurer; the Privy Council, upholder of the status quo, was gradually losing ground to the more reformist Parliament; the London merchants, backed by the City of London and Lord Mayor, had formed an alliance with the Welsh weavers. Generally the wool trade was depressed. When the Bill was debated, therefore, the argument went against the monopoly, despite the efforts of the members for Shrewsbury and Bristol, and the representations made by the Shrewsbury Drapers' Company. Although Parliament was adjourned and then prorogued before the Bill could be enacted, Privy Council followed the spirit of the debate and, in June 1621, declared the trade open. The Welsh were to be allowed almost complete freedom to sell their cloth to whoever they wished.

Strangely the real victors in 1621 were the Shrewsbury drapers, whose representative, once he recognised that the battle for the monopoly was lost, saw the opportunity provided by the Order: trade might now be free for the weavers but, when trade was low, there would be few buyers. The Shrewsbury Company had built its position through its ability to always find a buyer for the finished cloth in London. It could ensure the clothworker an income. Now, when trade was slack, Shrewsbury, by not purchasing elsewhere,

22

could use free trade to force the weavers to travel to its market. The effect of the 1621 Order was merely to remove the wool staple from Oswestry and place it, though not by 'right', in Shrewsbury.

This new development brought protests from both the North Wales clothiers and the citizens of Oswestry. Petitions were filed with the Privy Council in November 1621, April 1622, and two in June 1622, complaining that there was now no convenient weekly market, and of the time taken and expenses incurred in travelling to Shrewsbury. Furthermore, there was the matter of language—Oswestry was largely a Welsh-speaking town, whereas Shrewsbury was not—something which handicapped the weavers in their haggling. The clothiers demanded the return of the staple to Oswestry, but with freedom of all to buy. The Privy Council was once more sympathetic, and declared in favour of these new demands, admitting to "a general desire in the trade for the Oswestry market". The situation was hopeless, however, since the Shrewsbury drapers were too wily and too industrious in the protection of their interests. They made use of the rights of their recent opponents, Parliament, to attack the Privy Council decision, claiming that it went against both the will of Parliament and the law of the land. As ever in the wool trade, the drapers were the major source of wealth, and they, through a boycott of Oswestry market, could dictate their own terms, even to the Privy Council, whose members were told that the Company "do daily buy cloth in their own town and do refuse, as we are credibly informed, to repair to the market at Oswestry, and how to force them to go hither is not in our power . . ." So the Council admitted defeat, and once again set the trade free, clear in the knowledge that it would fall to Shrewsbury.

For Oswestry, the lifting of the monopoly and the move of the market to Shrewsbury was disastrous. In 1633 the town clerk wrote that "the town is much decayed and impoverished . . . Shrewsbury having ingrossed the said market". This must surely have been the case—Welsh wool was Oswestry's chief means of support in the 1530s when John Leland visited the town and presumably this had been so for many years beforehand. By Elizabethan times a monopoly situation had evolved, which had been recognised as a 'right'. It is almost certain that this market had generated a widespread prosperity and feeling of well-being in Oswestry, and the 16th and early 17th centuries had seen an expansion in Oswestry's size. The parish registers for this period indicate that there was also a sizeable local woollens industry, with weavers, dyers, walkers, shearmen and drapers amongst the men listed. These people would have escaped the worst effects of the changes, and would only have been inconvenienced in the same way as the rest of North Wales. However, those traders associated directly with the market would have suffered enormously, as after 1621 there would have been less money and fewer people passing through Oswestry. It is likely that many shops and several inns were forced to close, and that families had to move away in search of new employment. With the reduced number of tolls, the town's income would have dropped dramatically.

Thus Oswestry's fortunes fell as those of Shrewsbury rose. The town clung on to a small proportion of its trade, and even experienced a revival of business during the English Civil War, when the upheavals of the time loosened the Shrewsbury drapers' hold on the industry. Oswestry's fall had been largely in consequence of the Drapers' Company, so that, as the Company weakened in the 18th century, so Oswestry recovered, once more becoming the main market for Denbighshire cloth. In fact woollens remained an important feature at Oswestry market until well into the present century, though never again on the Jacobean scale; that circumstance had come about through chance, a chance which could not be repeated.

Civil War Battleground

Looking at the Castle Bank today it is very difficult to believe that Oswestry ever had a castle. The mound scarcely seems large enough, the stones on top seem far too few, and the general appearance of the place is of a large-scale rock garden or landscaped park. Though familiar with the Bailey Head and Castle Bank as names, the idea of 'Oswestry Castle' seems very strange. Nevertheless, Oswestry did have a castle, well built of stone and strongly manned, until just over 300 years ago. Modern Oswestry's misfortune is that our castle's demolition, in the Civil War, was much more thorough and total than that of Ludlow, for instance.

The castle was almost certainly a Norman foundation, built in the years immediately after the Conquest. Oswestry as a town goes back no further. In the 12th century, Madog ap Maredudd, Prince of Powys, added a tower—John Leland, the historian, noted that the castle still had a "Madog's tower" when he visited Oswestry in the 1530s. Oswestry was further fortified in the 13th century, by order of King Edward I of England, the builder of the great castles of North Wales, when the town walls were erected in the late 1270s. The four gates remembered today—New Gate, Beatrice Gate, Willow Gate, and Black Gate—were those of the original plan. The walls excluded the parish church from the town, enclosing the castle and its environs, the main streets and the market. The castle fitted into the walls between Beatrice and Willow Gates. Leland noted that the walls were about one mile in length, and that, apart from the gatehouses, there were no other towers.

Oswestry castle was often the scene of celebrations and pageantry. Parliament was adjourned here by Richard II in 1398, provoking the town's first royal charter as a result. A hundred years before this gathering, William Fitzalan, Earl of Arundel and Baron of Oswestry, received as guests Baldwin, Archbishop of Canterbury, and Giraldus Cambrensis, who wrote ". . . we slept at Oswaldestreo, that is Oswald's Tree, where we . . . were entertained by William Fitzalan, a young man of high birth and good education. His hospitality was truly English—most lavish and more magnificent and sumptuous than was seemly." However, the Fitzalans, prominent Marcher lords and influential royal counsellors, had other interests, lands, and castles. Increasingly they ruled through an appointed Constable. As Llinos Smith stated in 'Boroughs of mediaeval Wales'—"the castle provided a focal point, but it remained a modest structure and was never adapted to residential use by the lord."

Thus in the years leading to the Civil War and the military action labelled the 'battle of Oswestry' by William Cathrall, Oswestry castle and the town walls were in a sorry state, through many years of neglect and only occasional use. Luckily, a detailed report of their condition survives from this period, that of John Norden, who surveyed the Lordship of Oswestry for Thomas Howard, Earl of Suffolk, in 1602. Norden's report makes very interesting reading, and tells of municipal neglect of duty—the town burgesses being allowed £20 a year for repair of the defences yet being among the main defacers of them: as well as individual acts of what we would call vandalism, the castle walls were being used as a ready-to-hand source of faced building stone! Norden wrote "Richard Blodwalls servants with his teame carried divers dayes the stones by wayne-loads awaye, and Harry ap Thomas tooke a shiet of lead out of the same castle." He went on "it is a pittiful thing to see soe prety a pile soe defaced, and not fitt that the offenders should goe unpunished for they have taken downe whole towres and taken and carried awaye the stone, tymber, yron, and lead, throwne down the forewalle, uncovered the mayne towres, taken of the lead, carried away some of the tymber and the rest being uncovered rotts." The gates were "verye ruinous and decayed" and the walls were undermined, scaled, and "broken through at sundry places for doores." Presumably Suffolk reacted to this report, since he would not welcome any further deterioration to the fabric of his new Lordship. However, as we turn to the Civil War, and look at the final chapters of Oswestry's own military history, we should bear in mind the state of the town's defences.

Oswestry was Royalist at the start of hostilities, and declared for King Charles. The Lord Capel, the King's commander in the area, visited the town with a thousand horse to "fortify the town", telling the people to extend and strengthen the defences. Colonel Edward Lloyd of Llanforda raised a troop of dragoons at the cost of "all his plate", arming them at his own expense, "advancing likewise a month's pay to every soldier out of his own purse". Such actions—and the backing of the losing side—cost the Lloyds dear. The Colonel was Governor of Oswestry for a short time, but was replaced after a scandal. Lloyd's immediate opponent, the local commander of the Parliamentarians, was Thomas Mytton of Halston Hall, near Whittington, "a man well skilled in military art and of great personal courage". Mytton obviously know Lloyd from peace-time and, using this knowledge, he planned a trap for his rival. Lloyd was renowned for good living, so Mytton arranged for him to be invited out of the town one night to a dinner party, at which he would be arrested. Lloyd accepted, left the protection of the castle, and attended the engagement. However, the plot was discovered in time, and Lloyd escaped his captors and regained the safety of the town walls. The story spread, and he was replaced as Governor.

Oswestry anticipated a siege and the Royalists prepared for the struggle. Richard Gough of Myddle wrote that "the Governor of this Towne when it was a garrison for the King pulled downe many houses that were without the Wall lest they might shelter an enemy". The church steeple was pulled own, since its height could command the town. The bells were carried inside the walls and the organ was "imbezzled". Cathrall mentions a skirmish in March 1644 when Charles's nephew Prince Rupert "gallantly repulsed" an attack by Colonel Mytton and Sir Thomas Fairfax. However, the battle began in earnest in June 1644 when Mytton was joined by the Earl of Denbigh. Cannons were set up by the side of the church, and the New Gate was battered. The siege was short-lived, and victory and defeat quickly brought about. Cannonshot forced a breach in the wall and the infantry poured through into the town and on to the castle itself. Meanwhile, the New Gate was forced open through the daring of one George Cranage, who rushed the gate and broke the chains which were holding the drawbridge, thus allowing the cavalry to join their colleagues inside.

New Gate

More cannon and gunshot deterred the town's Royalist defenders from any hasty resistance, and forced their troops back along the streets up to the castle, closely followed by Mytton and Denbigh's 'Roundheads'. "In the rush to the castle some timorous men (Royalists) got over the walls, one broke his arm falling...", so reported the Earl of Denbigh's staff. The castle was then surrounded, and the castle walls were mined. Night fell before decisive action could be taken, but the following morning Cranage, "a bold and daring young man", was called upon again, to break down the castle gate. Gough mentions the deed in his 'History of Myddle', and an enlightening glance at 17th century warfare his report is : "being well lined with sacke (Cranage) was persuaded by the Generall to hang a buttar on the Castle gate. Now a buttar is an iron shell as bigge as a pott; it was filled with powder and wild-fire balls, and had a handle with a hole in it by which it might bee fastened with a nayle to any place. Cranage takes this buttar with a cart-nayle and an hammer, and gott from house to house unto the house next to the Castle, and then stepping to the castle gate hee fixed the buttar and stepping nimbly backe again, escaped without any hurt; the buttar burst open the gate."

27

The destruction thus caused brought things speedily to a close. The castle's garrison realised that further resistance was pointless, and their command negotiated terms of surrender. Thus the Royalists trooped out of Oswestry castle, leaving their weapons and powder behind. Inside were found "... 100 good muskets, besides others stolen away, eight halberts ..., one barrel of powder and suitable match, many swords and some few pistols". Two hundred soldiers were taken prisoner, along with "divers officers", and "twenty gentlemen of Wales and Shropshire". So the 'battle' of June 22nd and 23rd was over and, it now being Sunday, the victors immediately marched away to church. Colonel Mytton was next placed in charge of the captured castle, whilst Denbigh marched off to further action.

Thus Oswestry fell from Royalist to Parliamentary hands, and it was with Parliament that the town stayed for the duration of the struggle. An immediate attempt was made to recapture Oswestry for King Charles—the town was clearly thought of as important—and on June 29th a large force of several thousand men led by Colonel Marrow laid siege to the walls. Mytton, however, managed to get word to his kinsman Sir Thomas Myddleton of Chirk who was then camped with his troops at Knutsford. A quick march brought him to Halston, where he met and dispersed the Royalists, pursuing them "five miles towards Shrewsbury, to a place called Felton Heath".

Oswestry Castle's days were now sadly numbered, since Parliament soon decided that all such castles should be rendered undefendable, to prevent future resistance. As a result, the Parliamentary Survey of 1652 states, "the said castle is at present uninhabited, having lately been demolished". A good job of the demolition must have been done, too, looking at the few stones left today. The walls suffered a similar fate, surviving until just after the survey which recommended their destruction. The gate-houses lasted longer, standing for another hundred years and more. Today their sites—marked with slate plaques—and street names like Welsh and English Walls are the only real reminders we have of our tempestuous past.

Oswestry's Street Names

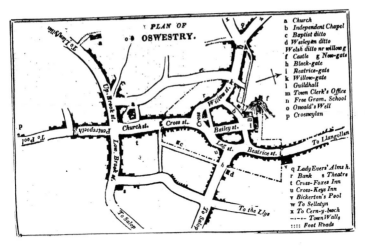

Town Plan, 1815

Taken at a purely functional level, street names are no more than guiding marks distinguishing one row of buildings from another. They are convenient labels which, together with house numbers, make the postman's task possible. Street names, however, pre-date the Post by many centuries, having proved essential wherever large groups of properties grew up, to help people to find their way about. Thus, in Oswestry, as elsewhere, many street names are of an obvious kind. Many refer to the town, village or landmark towards which the road leads: directional names such as Salop Road, Weston Lane, Church Street and Gobowen Road.

Nevertheless, names can refer to more than just places. They can relate to topical or historical events and personages; they can be purely fanciful; they can be chosen around some theme such as the tree names of the streets on the Carreg Llwyd estate. Towns are forever growing, their populations spreading out into new streets, avenues and crescents. The task of selecting names becomes more and more difficult, necessitating more and more inventiveness. However, names chosen are generally self-explanatory, both those adopted through council direction and those which have evolved through popular usage. Names adopted many years ago, however, have often lost their obvious meaning, and one of the most interesting facets of the study of street names is the explanation of this category. In Oswestry, Swan Lane at the bottom of Beatrice Street once led down to the Lower (or New) Swan Inn; today the street name and the frosted window pane facing onto the lane are the sole reminders of this feature of Oswestry's past. Similarly, the reason for the name Smithfield Street was until recently very clear, but now the street is stranded half a mile from the cattle market.

Perhaps in a hundred years' time names such as these might be useful to local historians, pointing out the location of the town's cattle market, or the site of the Swan. Much older examples of this phenomenon help us to identify the existence and lay-out of Oswestry's castle and walls—English and Welsh Walls, the Bailey Head, Bailey Street and Castlefields, illustrating how the town's fortifications were once scattered much more widely than the stump on the present-day Castle Bank might suggest.

It is evident that street names serve the local historian in at least two ways—they can throw light on a town's lay-out in times past, and they are themselves pointers to local historical figures, often chosen at random by a council desperately casting around for suitable sounding names. In Oswestry's case, there is a third possible use: to compare the Welsh-based names with the English, and hence to draw conclusions about our linguistic history. By looking at names such as Llwyn Road, Croeswylan Lane, the Clawdd Du, Penylan Lane, Brynhafod Road and Llys Lane, and comparing them with such English names as Bailey Street, Cross Street, and Beatrice Street, one can tentatively suggest that Oswestry had an English framework and was of English construction, but was peopled largely by Welsh speakers. This correlates with the evidence of parish registers, place names, and other written records. Thus in the 1620s Welsh weavers complained of having to sell their cloth at Shrewsbury rather than Oswestry, pointing out that they "not having the English tongue (were) forced to sell at a great loss"; the implication is that Oswestry was Welsh speaking.

Oswestry grew rapidly in the second half of the nineteenth century, the town's population rising from 4,817 in 1851 to 9,579 in 1901. The building styles of the Victorian period still dominate the town's appearance. A map of Oswestry dated 1815 mentions by name only Willow Street, Upper and Lower Brook Street, Cross Street, Beatrice Street, Leg Street, Bailey Street, the Cross and Pentrepoeth ("the burned part of the town"—a reminder of the 16th century fire which badly damaged the Pool Road area). Other streets were drawn in but not named, but even including these it is clear that Oswestry had grown little since the visit of John Leland in the 1530s. Oswestry's growth came with the arrival of the main-line railway, a fact which might explain why the town lacks the 'classic' Victorian names such as Inkerman Street and Alma Terrace; Oswestry waited until after the Crimean War before developing. The local council lacked nothing in patriotism, however, and throughout the years before the Great War the Royal Family was frequently called upon for street names: Albert Road, Victoria Street, Alexandra Road and Edward Street; more recently, Prince Charles Road and Windsor Close have continued this popular tradition.

Another area to explore was the town's history; St. Oswald was honoured, though King Penda, his conqueror at Maserfelth, was not. Stewart Road belongs to this category, and has an interesting derivation; it commemorates a tenuous link between Oswestry and the Stuart kings. After the Norman Conquest, the Oswestry area eventually fell to Alan FitzFlaad, thought to have been son or grandson of Fleance, son of Macbeth's victim,

Banquo. Alan had two sons. The elder, William Fitzalan, received Oswestry Castle, whilst the younger, Walter, became Steward to David I, King of Scots. This Walter the Steward, according to the story, was the founding father of the Stewarts or Stuarts.

Streets named after local celebrities, obviously well-known and well regarded once, can also seem alien now that the person honoured has been forgotten. Beatrice Street, Gatacre Road and, perhaps, Leighton Place fall into this category. Local landowners and notables were often celebrated in street names. Leighton Place, off Lower Brook Street, was part of the Sweeney estate in the 19th century. Lloyd Street and Hurdsman Street are further examples. The Gatacre family appears to have been well-liked locally, having its 'own' Avenue, Place, and Road. The family was not particularly local, hailing from Gatacre Hall, Claverley, but had married into the estates of the Lloyds of Drenewydd at the start of the nineteenth century. According to Isaac Watkin, the family still owned substantial lands locally in 1920. But what of the more obscure names? Beatrice Street leads down to the site of the Beatrice Gate, and William Cathrall thought that it was "named in compliment to Beatrice, the Queen of Henry IV". Henry had close contact with the area because of the Welsh rebellion inspired by Owain Glyndwr. However he married firstly Mary Bohun, and secondly Joan, widow of John IV, Duke of Brittany. Isaac Watkin put forward two other ideas—that the Beatrice in question was the wife of the fifth Earl Palatine or, more plausibly, that she was the wife of Thomas Fitzalan, Earl of Arundel, and the daughter of the King of Portugal. Thomas is thought to have built the Beatrice Gate. However, the picture is confused by the fact that 16th century writers spelled the name 'Betrych', or 'Betrige', 'Betris', and 'Beterich' and, fundamentally, by the inclusion of a 'Bader Strete' in a survey made of Oswestry in 1393. If this Bader Strete is the same as Beatrice Street, then the name predates all these Beatrices, and suggests another, unknown, derivation.

Albion Hill was, according to Watkin, named after the 'Albion' printing press introduced into his works on the Bailey Head by Samuel Roberts in the first half of the 19th century. This was Oswestry's first mechanical press. The name Carreg Llwyd reminds us that an ancient standing stone, probably of religious significance, stood in the fields next to the Shrewsbury Road before they were taken over for housing. Willow Street is difficult to explain, but it is believed that 'Willow' is a corruption of 'Gwalia', and that the Willow Gate was originally the Welsh Gate. The name Roft Street is derived from the name given to fields which previously lay to the south of the present thoroughfare. A map of 1795 calls the land 'Rofft-y-Sputty' suggesting that the land formerly belonged to some sort of hospital. This appears to have been the case; Eyton's 'Shropshire' refers to the foundation charters of the Hospital of St. John at Oswestry, and tells how Reynerus, bishop of St. Asaph, purchased land for a hospital, had it built, and later handed its running to the Knights Hospitallers of Halston. In the years after the Dissolution of the Monasteries, the Halston lands were granted, in 1560, to

George Lee of Shrewsbury, and included "one close of land called Croft-y-Spitty . . . in the township of Oswestry". A survey of Oswestry made in 1577 includes references to "Tho. Smaleman for divers parcelles of landes lying by the lower parke being part of the Chantry lands of the Lords called Croft Spitty" and "John Trevor for the rent of one croft called Crofte Deyspitell". One might assign Arthur Street to the Victorian royalty category, but that would be incorrect, since the name is recorded in the mid 18th century. Might it possibly celebrate Henry VIII's elder brother—Arthur, Prince of Wales—who died at Ludlow in 1502? Finally there is the strangely named Leg Street. The name is attested as far back as the reign of Edward II, when Edmund Fitzalan granted two shops there to the burgesses. At that time, and until comparatively recently, the street's shape resembled the Manx emblem—the Three Legs of Man : the two legs either side of the Queen's corner supplemented by present-day Cross Street.

Educational Origins

the foundation of Oswestry School

"The ancient Schoolhouse being very inconvenient and out of repair, it was resolved that a more spacious and suitable edifice should be erected." Thus, in quite a matter-of-fact way, the school, in a report dated 1830, explained its move to Cae'r Groes fifty years earlier. Since then, there has been steady expansion, which has become more rapid in recent times, so that today, the slopes are covered by a great rash of red brick. Increased size has facilitated increased scope.

Such growth seems paradoxical, when set against the record of the old school-house, which probably remained basically unaltered from the foundation of the school in the reign of King Henry IV, at the start of the 15th century, right up to 1776—a span of some 370 years. There can, however, be no definite proof of this, for though copies of documents relating to the original endowment survive, it is not precisely clear where the school-house was. The lych gate is dated 1631, and could well be earlier, whilst a beam within the school-house is inscribed 1634. A vertical beam on the east wall has been carved upon by scholars, for example "Francis 1660" and "Robert Owen of Landyn" (Mayor of Oswestry in 1686 and 1696). None precedes the seventeenth century, but a document from 1577 suggests that the property then in use had been occupied for some time, since it was in need of repair: "order was taken the 28th April Eliz. I XIX, for the disposition of ye woods growing upon the schoole lands to be from tyme to tyme ymployed to the use of the repar'con of the said Schoolehouse."

The "schoole lands" were not the lands around the school, but were the school's endowments, providing the income to pay the school-master, to keep the building in good condition, and to subsidise local boys' education. The school was founded on this basis by David Holbache, and after his death further land was added by his widow, Gwenhwyfar. These lands were probably in Sweeney, Treflach, Maesbury, and Crickheath. It was an ambitious plan and an original idea. The Dictionary of Welsh Biography describes the school as "the first of its kind in (what was then) Wales", while the Bishop of St. Asaph, at the school's anniversary celebrations in 1957, stated that Oswestry School was "probably the oldest purely secular school in the country, with an unbroken record." It is without doubt the longest-established grammar school in Shropshire, and it predates Shrewsbury School by 150 years. Winchester, nationally the first of all, was only set up 20 years beforehand.

This was the time of Falstaff and Prince Hal, of Hotspur and Owain Glyndwr. King Richard II had recently been murdered, probably at the orders of his cousin Henry, the first Lancastrian king. Agincourt was yet to be fought, the Wars of the Roses were decades away, whilst any ideas of a united Britain came only from Henry's half-hearted tilt at the Scots' crown. An Inquisition into the estates of the executed Richard Fitzalan, Earl of

Arundel, taken in 1398, shows that Oswestry Castle was no mean pile of stones, having a great chamber, wardrobe, constable's hall, butlery, kitchen, larder, and chapel. William Cathrall thought the list of articles recorded within was "a catalogue of mere rudeness, discomfort, and barbarity." This was the Oswestry about to receive one of the first grammar schools in the country, a town burned by the Welsh in 1400, and in 1403 the assembly point for Glyndwr's forces before the battle of Shrewsbury.

DAVID HOLBACHE'S WELSH DESCENT
(As given by Mr. Howell W. Lloyd)

Rhys Sais bore:
Argent a chevron inter 3 Boars' heads couped Gu. Tusked Or, and langued Az.

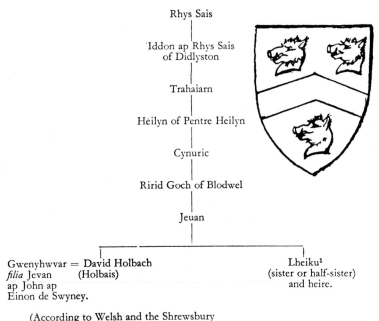

Rhys Sais
|
Iddon ap Rhys Sais
of Didlyston
|
Trahaiarn
|
Heilyn of Pentre Heilyn
|
Cynuric
|
Ririd Goch of Blodwel
|
Jeuan
|

Gwenyhwvar = David Holbach
filia Jevan   (Holbais)
ap John ap
Einon de Swyney.

Lheiku[1]
(sister or half-sister)
and heire.

(According to Welsh and the Shrewsbury Merchant Guild Roll he died *mortuus sine herede*).

[1] This may be the wife of Hastoun, sister or half-sister of David Holbache and daughter of Gwilim ap Einion Goch ap Grono of whom David bought land in Trevelech.

David Holbache was very much a part of this scene, coming as he did from an important Marcher family. He held high office under both Richard and Henry, seemingly avoiding their dynastic conflict, but he appears to

34

have been caught in the crossfire of the Welsh rebellion. Despite his English sounding name he was undoubtedly of Welsh ancestry, the son of Ieuan Goch ap Dafydd Goch ap Iorwerth ap Cynwrig ap Heilyn ap Trahaern ap Iddon. His mother Angharad was a direct descendant of Madog ap Maredudd, Prince of Powys. Owain Glyndwr, another descendant of this man, based his title 'Prince of Wales' largely on this link. Holbache was born at the Trayan, near Dudleston, which probably explains the entry in the Ministers' Accounts made in the reign of Edward VI, recording two gifts made by Holbache: "the service of a stipendiary founded of one priest to celebrate at the Altar of our Lady, within the parish Church of St. Martins, intended to continue for ever. The service of a stipendiary founded of certain lands and tenements heretofor given and enfeoffed by one David Holbache, to the use to have a priest to celebrate within the said parish Church of St. Martins to continue for ever." St. Martins benefitted in another way: the 1580 regulations of the school show that boys from Oswestry parish, or its pre-dissolution Chapelry, St. Martins, paid at lower rates — 4d entrance fee instead of 6d.

In a petition to Parliament in 1406-7 Holbache claimed that he had suffered great losses through the Glyndwr disturbances—2000 marks in rents, and over 2000 marks in destruction of property. He complained that he was both harried by Glyndwr's followers, and deprived of English citizenship. However this middle ground must have suited him well, for in difficult times he was certainly a survivor—a supporter of Richard II and a friend of Owain Glyndwr—who rode the upheaval of the usurpation and went on to greater office under Henry IV. He apparently trained in London as a lawyer, and he is first heard of in 1377, when he was appointed Crown Pleader and Attorney for both South and North Wales. He was evidently still with Richard II as his reign reached its climax, serving in 1399 on a Commission looking into forfeited Fitzalan monies in the Bromfield and Yale areas for the Crown, yet he remained in favour when the Fitzalans recovered their position under Henry IV, in Oswestry as elsewhere. He witnessed Thomas, Earl of Arundel's charter to the Town of Oswestry in 1407, and as late as 1418 his name appears on a document relating to the Fitzalans' Northamptonshire estates. Under Henry IV Holbache remained as Crown Pleader, was made War Treasurer for 1406, 1407, and 1408, and also became a Knight of the Shire, serving as Member of Parliament for Shropshire five times and twice for the borough of Shrewsbury. He appealed in Parliament for the removal of disabilities imposed on the Welsh after the battle of Shrewsbury, whilst, after gaining English citizenship, he tried to obtain from the King a grant of certain lands in Whittington forfeited by Ieuan ap Paynot, a supporter of Glyndwr. It is difficult to explain this double-standard towards the Welsh, Holbache's own ancestors; so much so that several writers have refused to accept the claim that, in 1415, he interceded with Henry V for Glyndwr's pardon.

However, there is more evidence to show that Holbache was indeed the founder of the Grammar School. The original documents have long since perished, but a seventeenth century copy has survived, which sheds some light on the actual foundation and the endowment of lands, though not, unfortunately, on the school or its curriculum. It is highly probable that the endowed lands were in Treflach, Sweeney, Crickheath and Maesbury. These were the areas detailed in a 1635 survey, in which two blocks of land in Sweeney are described as "Cae Holbage" and "Cae Holbage Vawr". A 1539 court case over non-payment of rent also mentions this "Holbadges land". Richard Oakley, in his 'History of Oswestry School', states that these field names survived at least into the nineteenth century. He suggests that this was the land given to Holbache as dowry for Gwenhwyfar by her father Ieuan ap John ap Eignon of Sweeney. It is also known that, earlier on, Holbache had paid rent to the Earl of Arundel, lord of the manor, for lands in Sweeney and Treflach. It has been argued that the "Holbadges land" was the initial endowment, made in 1404. After Holbache's death, it is likely that Gwenhwyfar handed over more lands—the mill at Maesbury included— with the clear instructions to the school's Trustees to keep to her late husband's intentions "that the rents issued and annual profits derived therefrom should be applied from year to year in the maintenance of one Schoolmaster in the Town of Oswestry." The actual dates are not entirely clear, having been obscured by time and poor copying. The documents are dated "6 H.IV" and "9 H.IV", or 1404 and 1407. However there is a discrepancy—Holbache is described as Gwenhwyfar's late husband, which in 1407 he clearly was not. Consequently, it is thought that the date for Gwenhwyfar's completion of the scheme should read "9 H.V." or 1421. This explanation seems reasonable.

The School's Trustees, those probably appointed by Holbache, are listed in this text, and they include such men to merit the description "the chief gentry of Shropshire and the Marches". There are nineteen names, including such local names as Sir John Hanmer, Thomas Lloyd, Edward Trevor and Thomas LeStrange. Three Trustees followed Holbache into Parliament, namely William Hord, Sir William Boerley, and John Wele. Two more, Richard Hova and David ap Thomas, are listed as "clerks"; possibly one was vicar of Oswestry parish. Several others were prominent local landowners or townsmen. John Wele was Constable of Oswestry Castle, afterwards Steward for the Earl of Arundel in Oswestry, and in 1413-4 he was charged by the King with the custody of Glyndwr's wife and family, in the city of London. William Hord, in 1416, was appointed Escheator of Shropshire and the Marches. Richard Ireland went on to become Receiver for the King of the Lordship of Oswestry and Shrawardine. Further names such as Cadwaller ap Owen, Evan ap Atha ap Evan, or Madoc ap David Gethin, strongly suggest that Holbache and Gwenhwyfar were far from being sole Welsh representatives.

Nevertheless, it has been argued that the foundation of the school was "intended to strengthen the English elements in the border country of Shropshire against the ever rebellious Welsh" (Leach's 'Schools of Medieval England'). This is possible, but appears to place too much emphasis on Holbache's petition for "Englishry", and on "English elements" amongst the Trustees. Richard Oakley put forward the opposite viewpoint, stating that he was "tempted to believe, although there is no proof, that Glyndwr had himself a finger in the pie, and may have been part instigator of Holbache's plan to found a school in Oswestry". Holbache and Glyndwr were certainly friends, being both lawyers trained at Thavies' Inn. Before Glyndwr's quarrel with his neighbour Reginald Grey of Ruthin, which escalated into a full-scale revolt against English rule, there had been no indication of Glyndwr emerging as 'Prince of Wales'. He had behaved like any other baron—receiving his education in London, serving the King in military campaigns, and attending the royal court. His involvement with the school could have been clouded by the revolt, but he can still be linked with several Trustees. Sir John Hanmer was his brother-in-law, who in 1404 represented Glyndwr in Normandy, where a treaty was signed by Charles VI of France supporting Welsh independence. Only in 1410 was Hanmer pardoned. Edward Trevor married Owain's niece, whilst both LeStrange and Holbache himself were more distantly related to the barons of Glyndyfrdwy. If this is the case, the school was perhaps founded to ease the 'Marcher problem', which Holbache had personally experienced, by helping to assimilate the Marches and Wales with English society. It was a Marcher solution to a problem caused by the very existence of the Marches, the problem of being neither Welsh nor English, which possibly characterises Oswestry to this day, and it was an attempt to bridge the gap between England and Wales through a common education system.

It has already been noted that nothing is known of the running of the school in the period of the foundation. In fact the earliest surviving material dealing with the teaching side of the school is dated 1577, by which time the duties of the Trustees had been taken over by the bailiffs and aldermen of Oswestry, along with the vicar of the parish. It is quite likely, however, that the curriculum would have changed much since Holbache's day, due to the declining use of French, for example, or as as result of the Reformation. Nevertheless by 1577, from the tone of the text, teaching appears to have been of a good standard, with the duties of the schoolmaster, laid down by the 'governors', wide-ranging. Item 6 stated that he should use his "best endevour to teach and instruct his Scholars to read and understand the Greek tongue, and shall read to them the common Authors in Latyn which be read in other Schools", whilst Item 7 continued, "he shall train his pupils in making vulgars, translating English into Latin, versfyinge, making of Epistells, Orations, and at least once a week to doe and write them up with their own hand", adding the comment "alway remembering that to write fair is for the Benefit of his Scholars". He was also instructed to teach those scholars bound for university the principles of logic. An usher was employed, who taught the younger boys "to read the A.B.C., the English primer and the grammar commonly called the King's Grammar". The cost of this education was fixed in 1580 at 2/- per annum, inclusive of the cost of entrance. It is difficult to imagine how a building the size of the old school-house could accommodate a school with such a curriculum. However, it is clear that smallness did not produce inertia or a poor school. The Grammar School might not have expanded at all for over 350 years, but it still built itself a good reputation and attracted the interest of Queen Elizabeth I (who granted the school forty shillings per annum), and Oliver Cromwell, who in 1657 personally wrote to the town's magistrates recommending a man of the necessary "piety and learning" for the vacant position of schoolmaster.

Edward Lhuyd, Celtic Scholar

Edward Lhuyd

Few people in the long history of the town of Oswestry have risen to national renown—statesmen, artists or soldiers for instance—and of those who have, only Wilfred Owen and Sir Henry Walford Davies are widely remembered today. Edward Lhuyd of Llanforda, considered "one of the foremost figures in the history of Celtic studies", who "ranked with the greatest antiquaries, naturalists and scholars of his time", is almost forgotten in present day Oswestry, when clearly he ought to be one of the town's most famous sons.

Edward Lhuyd was born in 1660, the illegimimate son of Edward Lloyd of Llanforda and Bridget Pryse of Glanfraid near Aberystwyth. He was the grandson of Colonel Edward Lloyd who commanded the Royalist garrison defending Oswestry in the Civil War, and he grew up at Llanforda Hall within an established Welsh border family, closely linked to Oswestry. Llanforda had been in the possession of the Lloyds for several hundred years, since the days of Meurig Llwyd who had distinguished himself in the Third Crusade, winning the right to use the imperial emblem (the double-headed eagle) which can still be seen on Llwyd Mansion in Cross Street. Meurig Llwyd gained possession of the estates of Llanforda and Llwyn-ymaen through his marriage to the heiress of Ieuan Fychan, constable of Knockin, and Llanforda remained in the family until 1685, when it was sold to Sir William Williams. The hall was rebuilt in 1780 by Sir William's descendants, the Williams-Wynns, who retained the estate into the present century. Llanforda Hall was finally demolished in 1949.

Edward Lhuyd was brought up in an atmosphere conducive to learning and investigation. His father was an enterprising man—involved in the Cardigan fishing industry, silver, lead and coal-mining, and market gardening—who took a personal interest in Llanforda's floral and kitchen gardens.

The estate was adorned with statues, fountains, rectangular flower beds and regular paths; exotic fruit and vegetables, such as artichokes and melons, were grown there. Lhuyd's family background was ideally suited to give him a good grounding in history, heraldry and genealogy: all traits carried on into his adult life. Lhuyd was educated firstly at Oswestry School, close to the parish church, and probably he taught there; he went up to Jesus College, Oxford in 1682. In Oxford he assisted at the newly-founded Ashmolean Museum, and in 1691 he was appointed Keeper of the Museum in succession to Dr. Robert Plot. He worked with fossils, plants and shells, and experimented with asbestos. He collaborated with his friend Dr. Edmund Gibson in the important task of revising the late 16th century 'Britannia' of William Camden. Gibson noted in his Preface, "When I tell you, that the whole business of Wales was committed to the care of Mr Edward Lhwyd, Keeper of the Museums in Oxford, no-one ought to dispute the justness and accuracy of the Observations".

The new 'Britannia' was published in 1695, the same year that Edward Lhuyd embarked upon his next project, which grew into his own great work, his 'Archaeologia Britannica'. Lhuyd's plan was to give "some account additional to what has been hitherto publish'd, of the languages, histories and customs of the original inhabitants of Great Britain; from collections and observations in travels through Wales, Cornwal, Bas-Bretagne, Ireland and Scotland". In Pembrokeshire he and his party were looked upon as conjurors, in Cornwall they were accused of being thieves, and whilst researching in Brittany they were arrested and imprisoned for eighteen days on suspicion of spying. The first volume—the "Glossography'—was published in 1707, and in this Lhuyd attempted to trace the original British language, comparing Cornish, Irish and Scots Gaelic, Breton and Welsh. In 1708 Lhuyd was elected a Fellow of the Royal Society. Unfortunately, he had no time in which to add further volumes to his work; in June 1709 he died of a cold which turned to pleurisy. He was buried in the 'Welsh aisle' of St. Michael's Church, Oxford.

Subsequent events have conspired to obscure Edward Lhuyd's achievements and worth. His manuscripts passed into private collections after his death and, over the years, a large proportion has been lost through fire. Llanforda Hall had passed out of the Lloyds' possession during Lhuyd's lifetime, and today the estate bears little resemblance to that Lhuyd would have known.

The Original 'Advertizer'

The first edition of the Advertizer came off the presses dated Friday January 5th 1849. Oswestry appears to have lagged behind other provincial towns in the matter of having a local newspaper—Shrewsbury's first was printed in 1772. The catalyst which produced the paper at this particular time was the railway, brought into Oswestry by the Shrewsbury and Chester Railway Company.

The Advertizer in its early days was markedly different from today's weekly paper in all respects except name. The Oswestry Advertiser and Railway Guide, as it was first known, began life as a monthly newspaper of a mere ten pages, and was much smaller in size, measuring only 6'' x 9''. It was printed and published by Samuel Roberts at his residence on the Bailey Head and the cover proudly proclaimed "guaranteed circulation one thousand copies". From issue no. 5 the Advertiser is priced at 1d, but the first issues give the impression of being free, paid for by the advertisments. Certainly Mr Roberts wrote, in issue no. 1, that "it is quite impossible to give a quantity of paper and printing away, unless the return from the advertising department compensates for the loss." The publisher, since he was first on the scene in Oswestry, clearly had to instil the idea of advertising in local tradesmen's minds; moving through the year 1849 one can watch the number and quality of the advertisements improve. Charges, by modern standards, were modest: 8 lines or under for 4/-, 20 lines for 7/-. Interestingly, in the first few months some advertisers appear to have doubted Mr. Roberts' circulation figures, since very soon he had to print an explanation: "in consequence of misconception respecting the extent of the circulation of the Oswestry Advertiser the Publisher deems it right to state that no more than half of the impression (1,000 copies) is distributed in the town. The remaining are circulated chiefly among the gentry and farmers residing within 10 miles of Oswestry; and a number of copies is forwarded regularly to the Solicitors, Auctioneers, and other gentlemen in the neighbouring towns."

Samuel Roberts was a bookseller by trade and, indeed, he used the pages of the Advertiser to publicise his new titles. One suspects that he filled up any vacant space in the paper with his own material in the first few months. Though journalism and newspaper publishing had long been closely associated with the book trade, it is clear that Mr. Roberts was no professional journalist. In issue no. 1 he displays a disarming candour about his new venture, as well as setting himself high ambitions—in the "Notices to correspondents" section, the closest the paper comes to a comment or editorial column, he writes that "our present publication is necessarily imperfect, and may possibly in some departments be erroneous. None who have ever endeavoured to collect information from original sources will be surprised at this, for they will know and appreciate the difficulties in the way of such research. We hope, by degrees, to fill out the defective, and correct the inaccurate departments; so as to approximate as nearly as may be to the

No. I. JANUARY.

[Guaranteed Circulation
One Thousand Copies.

THE

Oswestry Advertiser,

AND

Railway Guide.

OSWESTRY:

SAMUEL ROBERTS, BOOKSELLER, BAILEY HEAD.

MDCCCXLIX

The first issue of the Oswestry Advertizer

ideal we have set before us—'a complete compendium of useful local information' ".

Thus these first issues contain local information, placed by the advertisers, authorities and societies—the railway, the carriers, the coaches, shops, and schools—but there is nothing that the modern-day reader would call 'news'. It is unlikely, moreover, that Mr Roberts employed any journalist or reporter. The opening of the Cross and Powis Hall Markets, both in 1849, failed to feature in the pages of the Advertiser. In this sense, the early Advertiser was not a newspaper, but kept more to its name. However, news soon began to filter into the paper. Reports of local court proceedings were amongst the first items included, and the fulsome coverage of the question-and-answer sessions shows that the court case then as now had a wide appeal—knowledge of the people involved must add something to the interest! Poetry was occasionally included—the first poem printed being "Careg Llwyd, or Careg Lwyd, a conjecture", written about the standing stone then sited on the outskirts of Oswestry in fields by the Shrewsbury Road, which begins

"Whence art thou, hoary stone?—
Why cam'st thou here,—
By what hands brought,—
Say, in what bygone year?

The anonymous poet continues thus for several further verses!

The first edition of the Advertiser can be divided into several parts. Besides the title-page, there were nine sides of newsprint. Of these, two were taken by the Shrewsbury and Chester Railway and comprised a full timetable of the company's trains, along with details of connections and an explanation of the Oswestry service. As yet there was no line south of Oswestry, so from issue no. 2 the paper also included the coach services to Welshpool, Newtown, Ellesmere, Bangor and elsewhere. Another page was filled with an almanack of the month, which set out the saints' days, important events which had taken place on the various dates, gardening and weather hints, and astronomical detail, probably syndicated from another newspaper of the day. Four further pages were filled with advertisements, both local and national, and this number increased as the months passed. The final two sides were occupied by the Post Office's notices, the editor's column, details of carriers and fairs, and the court circuit.

It makes very interesting reading, and certainly seems much more of another age than do newspapers of a mere 25 years later. In 1849 newspapers were still liable to a stamp duty, paid per copy, though as a result papers received preferential rates from the Post Office. The train journey from Oswestry to Chester cost 6/- for first class travel, 4/4d second class, and 2/2½ third class, and took approximately one hour, longer than it does today (but from Oswestry rather than Gobowen). In any case, a foot-note to the notice indicates that speed was not thought all-important, though correctness was highly regarded: "Passengers to ensure being booked, should be at the principal Stations Five Minutes, and at the Roadside

Stations Ten Minutes earlier than the time fixed for the departure of the Trains, as the door of the Booking Offices will then be closed." Frustration must have been an accompaniment to rail travel then, too! More alien to modern eyes perhaps is the notice advertising the 'Royal Oak' coach service between Oswestry and the Bear's Head Hotel, Newtown. The trip took four hours, and fares were 11/- travelling inside, 7/- outside. The Post Office advised the reader on sending mail to North America: "the next Mails . . . will be transmitted from Liverpool on Saturday the 13th of this month . . . Postage 1s under ½oz. Newspapers 2d each."

The development of a railway network, and the improvement of roads and road transport were, by this time, making travelling between towns more convenient and regular. The villages, however, fared less well, unless they were fortunate enough to lie on the main routes, as did Rednal, Gobowen, Whittington, and Preesgweene. For the villages to the south and west of Oswestry, especially those in the hills, transport was limited to a weekly carrier service from the village into Oswestry for the market. Llanfyllin and Llanrhaeadr had a service into town on Saturdays as well as on Wednesdays, but places such as Meifod, Knockin, Llansantffraid, and Llansilin had only one carrier. It is ironic that this sense of isolation seems to be returning to the car-less of these areas today. The Advertiser of January 1849 included many notices for the carriers—the Llandrinio service from the Albion; Llangedwyn from the George; West Felton from the Horseshoe; Knockin and Kinnerley departing from the Three Tuns; Llanfechain from the White Horse. Many of these carriers' pubs have disappeared: the Green Dragon, The Coach and Dogs, the Albion, the Three Tuns demolished for the Cross Market, and the Horseshoe in Cross Street.

Issue no. 1 of the Advertiser included enough advertisements to justify the paper's title, several demonstrating their author's unfamiliarity with the genre. January 1849 saw notices for Miss Jackson's school in Willow Street, the Wesleyan Sunday School annual tea meeting, the Temperance & General Provident Institution, and Mr. Wynne's Black Gate Commercial School, which offered "Reading, Writing, Grammar, Geography, Arithmetic, Mensuration, Gauging, Book-keeping, &c" at 15/- per quarter, inclusive of stationery and books. William Corney, confectioner of Cross Street, wished "to inform his friends that he (had) a supply of Plain and Ornamental Sponge, Plum, and other Cakes, suitable for the present season, as Twelfth Night Cakes". Samuel H. Coombes, boot and shoe dealer, claimed that "Feet deformed by gout or nature fitted with ease and comfort", whilst another advertisement propounded the virtues of "Plumbe's genuine arrow root, prepared by the Native Converts at the Missionary Stations in the South Sea Islands".

The publisher himself did not need convincing of the merits of advertising, and from the first he used his newspaper to promote his other activities, such as the 'Standard Book and Magazine Library': a forerunner of the public library system, a subscription circulating collection of books "comprising some of the best works in every department of literature, and the leading Reviews and Magazines of the day." Mr Roberts pointed out that a full catalogue was in preparation, and that a recent addition to stock was "Mr Dickens's Christmas Book—'The Haunted Man and the Ghost's Bargain' ". The collection of magazines available was excellent, and included Blackwood's, Fraser's, Punch, the Edinburgh Review and the Mirror. Such clear signs of a highly literate reading public in Oswestry make the late arrival of a local paper puzzling, especially since Samuel Roberts was so obviously apprehensive about his venture, and seemingly not at all sure what exactly to expect from it.

That the paper flourished and lives on today is justification and vindication for the publisher's faith. How much the Advertizer owes its success to its early years cannot be gauged. However the paper's rapid growth in size, frequency and scope, and the immediate reaction from advertisers and letter-writters, indicates that there was a market outside the confines of the Shrewsbury and Chester Railway waiting to be tapped.

An Electoral Upset

Without any doubt, the 1904 parliamentary by-election for the Oswestry constituency was remarkable. It was an election campaign reported day-by-day in the columns of The Times, with the final result the subject of editorial comment. It was a campaign which involved the Prime Minister of the day (Balfour) and prominent Members of Parliament such as Joseph Chamberlain and Winston Churchill, and which saw the latter speak at both Ellesmere and the Powis Hall Market in Oswestry. The count brought such large crowds to the Bailey Head that it was thought best to announce the results in private. Above all, the campaign was noteworthy in that it produced a Liberal victory. Such are the bare bones of the story of the by-election which took place in the summer of 1904, whose result denied the Tories a clean sweep of the election victories over the last 100 years.

The constituency, properly known as West Shropshire, then ran south from Oswestry and Ellesmere to Minsterley, Snailbeach, Pulverbatch and Pontesbury. It was a large seat, and one which was die-hard Conservative territory, occupied periodically by the Leighton and Ormsby-Gore families and, in the late 19th century, often uncontested. In 1900, Stanley Leighton had been returned without a fight, whilst the 1901 by-election, caused by his death, had given the Hon. George Ormsby-Gore 56.3% of the vote and a majority of 1,088 over A. H. Bright, a Liverpool Liberal. On June 26th the second Baron Harlech had died after a prolonged illness, and his son moved from the Commons to the Lords, leaving the seat vacant once more. Both the Conservatives and Liberals were ready with a candidate and the election was quickly set for Tuesday July 26th. The heavy weight of tradition inevitably led to a certain over-confidence in the Tory camp—the Government might be unpopular nationally, but defeat in Oswestry itself was a concept rarely considered throughout the campaign. Thus, in early July, The Times correspondent reported a "growing feeling that (the Conservative) majority will be much larger than was at first anticipated". Reality was far less settled.

What then of the candidates—the Conservatives' William Clive Bridgeman and the Liberals' Allan Heywood Bright? Bridgeman was a constituency man by birth; his father was the Hon. J. Bridgeman, rector of Weston-under-Lizard, and the candidate himself hailed from Leigh Manor, Minsterley. However, despite his Shropshire roots, he had received his education at Eton and Trinity College, Cambridge, before serving as private secretary to Lord Knutsford and then Sir Michael Hicks-Beach—prominent Unionist M.P.s in the 1890s; at the time of the campaign, Bridgeman was a member of the London County Council. In contrast the Liberal, Bright, came from Liverpool, where he was a ship-owner and involved in the iron and tin-plate trades. He was two years older than Bridgeman, being born in 1862, and he too had had a public school upbringing, at Malvern and Harrow. He had contested Exeter in 1890 and 1900, and had run against

46

the Conservatives in the 1901 Oswestry by-election. Subsequently he had been re-adopted as Liberal candidate, and had bought Brookside, Bronygarth, as his country residence. In a sense he was more of a local figure than Bridgeman, especially in the northern part of the constituency.

A. H. Bright and family

Local links can have a great bearing on an election's outcome, and the Border Counties Advertizer, at the outset of the campaign, saw that Bright was much better placed than previous Liberal challengers: "We have always held and declared that to suppose a Liberal candidate could come down on the eve of an election and capture a seat which has been held by the Conservatives for over half a century is absurd. It is a very different thing, when a candidate, and one of Mr. Bright's quite unusual merits, with great good sense, regards his first inevitable defeat as merely the beginning of the fight, and carries on a strenuous battle for the space of three years, visiting many parts of the constituency where political meetings were almost unknown." In a sense, the Liberals had taken over the role of sitting tenant, and the true 'local man', Bridgeman, had to try to regain the lost ground. In this struggle, he was not aided by an outbreak of north-south rivalry within the local Conservative Association, which had seen the southern section defeat an Oswestrian move to select another Ormsby-Gore as their candidate. The south pushed through the candidature of Bridgeman, who had no real link with Oswestry, the principal town in the constituency. Clearly this affected the way in which local Tories went about their canvassing and,

47

throughout the contest, the Liberals seemed to out-do their opponents in this department.

Nationally the Conservative Government, led by Arthur Balfour, was under attack on several fronts, and by the Spring of 1904 it had already suffered several by-election reverses. The national swing to Liberalism, which in the 1906 election reduced the Conservatives to a mere 132 M.P.s (with an additional 25 Liberal Unionists) had already begun, and the resultant feeling pervaded the Oswestry campaign. This, added to the Tories' local problems, certainly weakened Bridgeman's position. The Tories were in a dilemma; Oswestry was regarded then, as now, as a safe Conservative seat, but in the heady atmosphere of 1904 it was seen as vulnerable. However, the Conservatives were guarded in their activity, probably believing that too much ground-work would be seen as a sign of worry and pessimism. The Liberals, on the other hand, threw everything into the fight, in much the manner that they contested by-elections in the declining days of the Heath government of the 1970s. The Times of July 8th 1904 reported that the Liberals had flooded the constituency with "special organisers", and, as polling day approached, West Shropshire was invaded by a stream of M.P.s of both parties. Thus Winston Churchill and Ivor Guest, both of whom had just left the Conservative benches over the issue of tariff reform and protectionism, visited the area. In addition, a number of pressure groups set up temporary offices in the town, and lent their support to the candidates.

It is worth noting the number of local and national bodies which played a part in the election. Bridgeman could count on the backing of the Shropshire Licensed Victuallers' Association, the National Trade Defence Fund (another licensees' body), the Tariff Reform League, the Rural Labourers' League, and the National Conservative and Unionist Temperance Association. Bright was supported by the Free Trade League, the Free Church Council, the Oswestry Labour and Trades Council, and the Free Licensed Victuallers' Association. National affairs were carefully weighed for their local impact, and local bodies fought for their own point of view. Both candidates were questioned on the contentious issues of the day by these groups, and won or lost support according to their replies. Certainly the national and local press attached great importance to these groups, and their moves were regularly reported, but it is true that, in finely balanced contests, the allegiance of any group of voters can gain an inflated significance, and this was probably the case in 1904.

Bearing this in mind, the by-election came at an unfortunate time for the Government, since national affairs were rife with controversy. The Licensing Bill was then passing through Parliament, and licensees from local free houses feared it would jeopardise their livelihood; a recent court case, the Taff Vale judgement, had posed a threat to trade union rights, and had alienated many working class voters, who also objected to the Government for sanctioning the importation of thousands of Chinese coolies into South Africa to work almost slave-like in the Transvaal gold-mines. Furthermore, the Education Act of 1902 had integrated the voluntary non-conformist schools into the mainstream education system, and provoked some non-conformists to withhold their education rates, notably in parts of Wales, where the parson and the schoolteacher might be the only Anglicans in the village. Lloyd George and the veteran Baptist preacher Dr. Clifford were among those who opposed the Act, and it was certainly an issue in the by-election, with Dr. Clifford making several speeches in favour of Bright.

However, the major issue nationally was tariff reform. This had caused the recent defections from the Tory ranks, and eventually it was this which so weakened the Conservative party before the 1906 general election. Tariff reform was the baby of Joseph Chamberlain, Birmingham businessman and, until 1903, Colonial Secretary, and it meant two things—duties on imported goods to protect British industry, and preferential tariffs for the Empire, to strengthen colonial bonds. The idea appealed to British industry, under pressure from German and American rivals, but went directly against free trade theories. Fundamentally it threatened dearer foods. Chamberlain argued that protection would safeguard British jobs and help industry, but the Liberals made political capital out of the threat to prices. Oswestry gained in significance from the clear contrast between candidates: Bridgeman was a 'whole-hogger' backing Chamberlain to the hilt, whereas Bright was a traditional free-trader, who, in his election address, claimed that "this (protection) means dear food, dear clothing, dear living, and general suffering . . . it means higher rent for the landlord and larger profits for some manufacturers", and also that "Mr Bridgeman will doubtless deny that his programme is Dear Food and Cheap Labour, more poverty for the Poor, and more riches for the Rich, but he cannot contradict the facts . . ." Bridgeman countered with the slogan "tariff reform means work for all".

It might have been noticed that, although the election was a straight fight between Liberals and Tories, with no Labour candidate, issues were not unlike today's and the debate no less heated. The Labour party in Oswestry waited until 1918 before putting forward its own candidate, but it should not be imagined that the working class vote was unimportant in preceding elections. It has been seen that the Oswestry Labour and Trades Council voted to back Bright. This was important: the labour vote was vital, with the constituency more noticeably industrial in 1904 than it is today. In 1904 there were large work-forces at the Cambrian Railways, Ifton Colliery, and the mines in Hanwood and Pontesbury. Both candidates appreciated the potential value of the labour vote, but clearly Bright, who was quite a radical, held the advantage. Bridgeman did not shy from working class areas, but he had little success in them. He "met with some opposition" when speaking to the Stiperstones and Pontesbury miners, and the Advertizer of July 20th reported "the protectionists' visit to Cambrian railwaymen" noting that "there was quite a delightful little meeting near the Cambrian Railway Works on Saturday. The railway men knocked off work for the week at noon, and between them and a well earned dinner interposed Mr. Wynne Corrie (of the local Conservative Association and Park Hall), Mr

Bridgeman, and Col. Kenyon-Slaney (M.P. for Newport) backed by a posse of police led by Sgt. Lewis". The Times reported "much good-humoured heckling". However, it was well-informed heckling, with pertinent questions asked on issues such as tariff reform and the Transvaal's Chinese workers. Bright later acknowledged the support he had received from the railwaymen.

The Times was Conservative and protectionist, and the Advertizer was no more objective, being undeniably Liberal, extolling Bright's virtues and constantly pointing out the Tories' deficiencies. On July 6th it led with the headlines "Bright this time", the Liberals' clever slogan, and "Mr Bridgeman's programme: dear food and cheap labour". Events were reported from a Liberal standpoint, and when the result had been announced the paper proudly printed the comments of the Welsh Gazette: "The Oswestry Advertizer did yeoman work, not only during the contest, but throughout the lean and barren years when success seemed a mere mirage on the far horizon. That paper was calm, strong, enlightened, scrupulously fair, and, above all, consistent". Possibly new ground was broken, too, by the insertion of a photographic supplement in the copy of July 6th, which showed the Brights at their Brookside home, and at the wheel of their new 10 h.p. Wolseley car.

Inevitably it was a hectic campaign, with such a number of participants and such a range of issues. Speech-making was still very important at the local level—more so than is the case today, when the debate is largely television-based and between the party leaders. The newspapers carried daily bulletins of the candidates' progress around the constituency and each day's speeches reflected upon, and reacted to, those of the day before. There were countless meetings; in the final week both parties held between 40 and 50, with additional rallies by the Free Trade and Tariff Reform Leagues. Interestingly, Mrs. Bright both accompanied her husband on his travels and addressed meetings on her own, several years before women's suffrage.

The election was to take place on Tuesday July 26th, and as the day approached so the tension mounted. Both sides became increasingly wary of predicting the result, as both wished to maximise their support. The Advertizer of the 27th — published before the result was announced — reported that "excitement seems to have reached fever heat on Saturday when interrupted meetings and street fights were conspicuous for their frequency". Bridgeman received a letter from Chamberlain and a telegram from Balfour, the Prime Minister, the texts of both missives being published in The Times. A close result was expected, but the Liberals, who had conducted a fine campaign, retained their trump card until the last minute, and on election eve Winston Churchill and Ivor Guest arrived to speak at the Powis Hall Market, having been driven on from Ellesmere. The meeting was described as "a magnificent demonstration for free trade"—free trade songs were sung, and Churchill was greeted with "ringing cheers". Speeches were strongly worded and committed; Churchill said that "there was no doubt about the issue which was at stake, and Mr Bridgeman was to be congratulated on not having sought refuge in these shufflings and equivocations which were so dear to the heart of the Prime Minister. Mr. Bridgeman had come forward boldly and brutally as an avowed protectionist. The first issue they had to consider was protection versus free trade, but there was another issue—whether the time had not arrived when they should have another kind of government, for what they had had during the last four years was not Conservatism but reaction."

Election day brought frenzied activity. Both candidates toured the twenty four polling stations, and both parties worked hard to ferry their supporters to the polls. Bright had twenty cars available, more than Bridgeman, but the Tories had more carriages. Altogether, around three hundred vehicles were put to use "from motorcars and roomy wagonettes to dog carts." As is the case today, the result was delayed until the following lunch-time, and in this election the result understandably generated great interest. Crowds filled the Bailey Head—so much so that it was thought advisable to announce the result in private to prevent trouble. However, the news spread quickly through the crowd—the Liberals had won! Bright amassed 4,542 votes to Bridgeman's 4,157; and the celebrations began. Bright toured the constituency in his Wolseley, thanking the villagers. The Daily News reported that "the country is as deeply stirred as the towns" and concluded that the Conservatives were losing their grip on even the supposedly 'safe' areas. Various explanations were given for the result. Bridgeman blamed the fear of dearer food. Bright claimed that "the people had risen up against the Government. They objected entirely to the way in which the interests of the people had been sacrificed to the selfish interests of a few" and said that he could not remember ever seeing "such popular feeling for Liberalism". "Shropshire was sick unto death of the domination of the Tory squires", he said, adding that Bridgeman "was a good man but. . . he had little chance because his cause was a bad one." Clearly local Conservatives blamed themselves to some extent, and no more than 10 days after their defeat The Times reported that, though Bridgeman had been re-selected as their candidate, the local Tories had also taken steps "to reorganise the party in the division". In fact, it was a combination of many things which produced the upset. The Liberals conducted an excellent campaign and had a good candidate. Nationally the Government was in decline, and split by the tariff reform issue; Balfour had introduced several unpopular measures of the sort which could not win votes. The local Tories were disunited, with a man who could be portrayed as an 'exremist' as their candidate.

So much then for 1904. Oswestry was in the forefront of national affairs for a short time, and at the National Liberal Club's annual reception the mere word 'Oswestry' was enough to raise many a cheer. Undoubtedly the result was bad news for the Government, and even The Times admitted that the result "was a legitimate cause for rejoicing" for the Liberals. For Oswestry, however, 1904 was surprise enough, for in 1906 the seat reverted to the Tories, directly against national trends! Bridgeman replaced Bright, and Conservative Oswestry has remained ever since. Bright enjoyed but two years in the Commons, though he fought two subsequent elections at Stalybridge in an attempt to get back in, before leaving politics for good. Eventually he moved from Bronygarth to Herefordshire, where he lived, working on mediaeval English literature, until his death in 1941. Bridgeman's future was very different—he rose higher and higher, serving as Oswestry's M.P. until 1929, becoming Secretary for Mines in 1920, Home Secretary in 1922, and First Lord of the Admiralty in 1924. Ironically, during this time he became a Cabinet colleague of Churchill, his vehement critic in 1904. He was created 1st Viscount Bridgeman, became a Privy Councillor, was President of the M.C.C. in 1931, and Chairman of the B.B.C. in 1935, the year he died. The two candidates, rivals in 1904 and 1906, moved on to contrasting lifestyles, and the local Liberal party declined so quickly from its highpoint of 1904 that in the election of 1918 no candidate was even put forward.

Pubs, the Past, and the Demon Drink

It is indicative of Oswestry's market town status that the town possesses so many inns. There are over thirty public houses to serve a population of just 12,000, showing how much Oswestry is dependent for its prosperity upon money brought into the town. This situation has existed as least as far back as the 16th and 17th centuries, when the custom of the weekly wool market would have been important to many inns and taverns. Even after the woollen trade declined in the early 17th century a cloth market remained, if on a much smaller scale, and the livestock and produce markets carried on unimpaired. Several inns survive from this period; a search through the local parish registers reveals the existence of the Sun in 1672, the Bell in 1663, the Star in 1683, the Red Lion in 1668 and the Fox in 1687. It is highly probable that these inns all date back further still, before either the Restoration or the Civil War.

It is clear that Oswestry had far more pubs 200 or 300 years ago than it does today. In the past there were fewer restrictions placed upon the licensed trade, and it was less difficult to open up a new inn. Many inns had only a short existence, opening and closing as trade ebbed and flowed. As a result, Oswestry has seen many different pubs—almost a hundred since the 1770s— with such names as the Talbot, the Hog and Armour, the Leopard, and the Plume of Feathers. Success or failure depended upon several factors: the pulling power of the market was always crucial, but, towards the end of the 18th century, the general improvement in the communications network became a second important factor. In the early years of the 19th century, the Cross Keys Hotel profitted from the routing of the London to Holyhead mail coaches through Oswestry, and the Wynnstay Hotel enjoyed prosperity from this same source.

Oswestry's town walls had been pulled down in the aftermath of the Civil War, but the four gates remained intact for a further 100 years; the Black Gate was demolished in 1771, and New Gate, Beatrice Gate and Willow Gate all disappeared from the streets in 1782, the gates' survival long after their purpose had gone being indicative of the stagnation of Oswestry once the wool trade had moved away. By 1815 the town was pulling out of this slow decline, but Oswestry was still much the same size as it had been during the reign of James I, or even at the time of John Leland's visit in the 1530s. Only along Salop Road had there been any real expansion. However, when 'progress' did arrive it acted with speed—Oswestry was transformed during the reign of Queen Victoria. Like everything else, the town's inns felt the change, particularly in three distinct but inter-related spheres.

Whilst most of the continent of Europe was embroiled in revolution, and as ten years of Chartist agitation was coming to an unsatisfactory conclusion in London, Oswestry was experiencing its own, less violent upheavals. The key dates were December 23rd 1848, when the Shrewsbury & Chester Railway's branch line from Gobowen to Oswestry opened, June 6th 1849 when the Powis Hall and Cross Markets began trading, and

July 4th of the same year when business commenced at the Smithfield and Horsemarket. This six month period laid the foundation for a half-century of great change, which re-shaped a major part of the town, and caused the town's centre of gravity to swing away from Willow Street (which was already in decline) towards the railway and the Smithfield market. In terms of inns, the Duke of York, Owen Glyndwr, Mitre and Woolpack disappeared from Willow Street, whilst in contrast Salop Road and Beatrice Street prospered. The Barley Mow, Freemasons' Arms, Smithfield, Bricklayers' Arms, and Black Lion all opened up in Salop Road, and a cluster of inns—the Lower Swan, Crown, Volunteer, and Railway—sprang up at the foot of Beatrice Street. Names chosen, like the Mechanics' Arms, the Cambrian Inn, and the Engine and Tender, reflected their times, just as, in earlier days, names such as the Woolpack and the Coach and Horses had reflected theirs.

The Coach and Dogs

A second consequence of the new prosperity was the demolition of many interesting old buildings, and the radical alterations of several more. The Greyhound, and the Five Bells were transformed from brick and timber cottages into substantial red-brick inns, in a similar manner to the Sun, which was completely re-built in the 1880s. In his 'Personal reminiscences of Oswestry fifty years ago', published in 1904, Mr T. Owen described the

54

old Sun as "a house much frequented by country farmers . . . a low-roofed rambling old structure, the ground floor being a step below the street level. It was built of brick and timber, and the exterior walls, being always kept nicely white-washed, presented a quaint and pleasing object to the eye". Nearer the town centre the White Horse Inn, now a chemist's shop, was refronted in 1872, though the horse's statue is a retention from the previous building, and is apparently derived from a heraldic device which adorned the New Gate, which formerly stood nearby.

The third phenomenon was the emergence in Oswestry of a strong and highly influential temperance movement, which grew up through the desire to act against public houses such as the Horseshoe, which was located opposite the Cross Keys at 12 Cross Street. This particular inn commenced business in 1828, and survived until the 1870s. It had a reputation for rowdiness from the start: Mr Owen claimed that there were frequently "ghastly street fights . . . owing to the stimulating drinks sold within". Undoubtedly the Victorian public house was a very different establishment to the comfortable inns of the present day. Pubs were rougher, more numerous and sold stronger ales. Drink was at the root of many a social problem, and had a powerful hold over the working community.

Locally the driving force in the temperance campaign was the curiously named Oswestry Public House Company. This body, which had its head-quarters in the Harlech Castle in Oswald Road, bought up public houses in the town in order to close them down. It is interesting to note that Oswald Road, now the main link between the railway station and the town centre, boasts no pub in its entire length. This might appear strange, since the coming of the railway in 1848 had attracted several new inns at the foot of Beatrice Street. However, this first railway line terminated off Station Road, just down from Beatrice Street; Oswald Road came later, in the wake of the building of the Cambrian line at the start of the 1860s, and it was graced not by inns but by two temperance hotels—Matthews' Commercial Hotel and the Harlech Castle. This contrast reflects the growing strength of the local temperance movement over these years.

Nevertheless, even a cause as honourable as temperance had its opponents. Those with a vested interest in the licensed trade obviously had objections, but there were also those who suspected temperance of less than altruistic motives. In the 1840s a local printer produced the following verse, which demonstrates that feelings were running high:

A Teetotal Song, by a Shropshire Collier (late a Tee-Totaller).
To the old Chewn of 'Gee O Dobbin'—

Success to the Farmer, the Plough, and the Flail,
He sends me good Barley, to make me strong ale;
No longer I'll go to the TEE-TOTALSHOP,
So farewell 'old Samson', 'Long Life', and such SLOP.
    Gee, O Dobbin, &c.

I've empty'd my Pockets too long with such Stuff,
And many more of it have had quite enough;
Thro' Slops which I've Guzzled, and eating of 'Snacks',
My Children and Wife have scarce Rags to their Backs.
  Gee, O Dio, &c.

My body got weaker, (O, true is my Tale)
But now I'm reviving, by drinking good Ale;
It does me more good, and takes from me less Cash,
Than starving my Guts with the Tee-Total Trash.
  Gee, O Billy, &c.

(and so on, through several further verses)

Despite counter attacks like this, the temperance movement made the second half of the 19th century a period of retrenchment for the licensed trade.

Temperance was responsible for the fall of some of the most notable inns in Oswestry. The Coach and Dogs, established as an inn in around 1660, was bought "for philanthropic purposes" in the Spring of 1882 and converted into a cocoa house. The Smithfield Inn in Salop Road became the Black Gate tea rooms, and the Duke of Wellington in Bailey Street became another temperance hotel. Arguably the finest of all was the Three Tuns, a half timbered building which stood back behind Bailey Street, on a site now covered by F. W. Woolworth's store and New Street. William Price, in the history of Oswestry published in 1815, stated that the house "in former days was the principal inn of the town, and the chief resort of the drapers. The feast of St David is annually celebrated in this venerable mansion, which is usually attended by most of the gentlemen of the town and neighbourhood." Several of the inn's windows had been engraved with a coat of arms and heraldic devices, and the dates 1604 and 1640 had been carved in the woodwork. In 1880 the property was purchased by the Oswestry Public House Company and converted to temperance as the Oswestry Castle. Sadly the building was demolished at the start of the present century to make possible the extension of the Cross Markets.

The number of inns has continued to fall in the 20th century, though the temperance lobby has given way to government legislation and tighter official controls. The Old Swan in Beatrice Street, which had existed as an inn since the 16th century, was pulled down in the 1930s. The Woolpack and the Fighting Cocks, both long established public houses, also closed down (though thankfully closure did not mean demolition). Today Oswestry has no brewery of its own, when once there were several. There has been much change—the licensed trade is constantly changing—but, overall, Oswestry's present-day licensee, catering for the local community, the market traders, and the passing travellers, earns his income in a very similar manner to the innkeeper of the 17th century.

Oswestry Against England

a sporting milestone

Oswestry Town Football Club, a member of the Northern Premier League since 1979, has had a long and chequered history. The side has played in many different leagues, looking at various times to the north, south, east and west in its allegiance. They have progressed from the Shropshire League and the Welsh National League, through the Lancashire Combination into the Birmingham, Cheshire County, and Southern Leagues. They have collected trophies along the way, winning the Shropshire Senior Cup on several occasions, and the Welsh Cup three times—in 1884, 1901, and 1907. Though Oswestry has never really hit the football headlines, the club has a creditable record stretching back to the early years of organised football. The Welsh Football Association was founded in Wrexham in 1876, and Oswestry was one of the founding members, keeping up this membership to the present day. Indeed, in the years before the Great War, Oswestry was a powerful force in Welsh football, providing Wales with many players of international standard. At this time the game of football was still young, the rules were but recently recognised, and governing bodies were only newly set up. As yet there was no Liverpool, no Arsenal, and Manchester United was only founded in 1880 as Newton Heath. League football was a thing of the future (the Football League was not formed until 1888) but Oswestry played regularly, arranging 'friendly' fixtures in the manner of many present-day rugby and hockey clubs, against such teams as Wednesbury Strollers, Wolverhampton, Ruabon, and Whitchurch.

Wales played its first international fixture in 1876, against Scotland, and from the start Oswestry was represented. Annual matches with the Scots continued from this time with little success initially, but no challenge went out to England until 1879. The match which resulted from this challenge saw England triumph in a closely-fought tie, played under atrocious conditions; but Oswestry's interest lies inevitably with the Welsh side, and with its unusual composition. For in 1879, on January 18th, Oswestry supplied nine of the eleven Welshmen who faced the might of England at the Kennington Oval. The Oswestry Advertizer and Montgomery Mercury of January 15th 1879 commented : "The English may be said to be a thoroughly representative eleven, the players being chosen from the two universities and the leading association clubs, viz. Sheffield Wanderers, Clapham Rovers, Notts, and Remnants. The Welsh Association have, however, selected all the players save two from the Oswestry club...", the side lining up being "Goal, G. Glascodine; backs, Ll. Kenrick (captain), and G. G. Higham; half-backs, W. Williams and T. Owen; right-side, W. H. Davies and W. W. Shone; left-side, D. W. Owen and J. Roberts (Llangollen); centre, D. Heywood and J. Price (Wrexham)". It appears that soccer was a more attacking game then than it is today, with Wales including six forwards to four backs.

It might well be pointed out, for fairness' sake, that the Welsh selection committee met at the Queen's Hotel in Oswestry. One might even suspect a little bias, but that matters little now. What is important is that a small club like Oswestry provided these nine Welshmen to travel south with their two colleagues and face players who had appeared in F.A. Cup finals—a team which had defeated the Scots (something the Welsh team was not to do until 1905). Questions about the team selection were asked at the time—notably from the Wrexham area—but, in the event, the team performed very creditably.

Wales was certainly not over-confident. Success, in fact, was scarcely even considered before the match. The aforesaid Advertizer report stated "a practice match (has been) arranged for Thursday afternoon, at four o'clock, on the Ruabon ground, when it is most essential that all the players should be present, as to meet so formidable a team as England without being properly organised will, we fear, be simply ridiculous". Organisation, however, was such that the party did not leave for London until the last train on the Friday night! Weather in the capital on the Saturday was far from ideal : "the ground was covered with snow, while a mixture of snow and sleet fell during the greater part of the game". The poor conditions clearly affected the size of the crowd, which was far below that of present-day international fixtures; on this wet and windy day in 1879 less than one hundred people turned up to watch! The weather was to prove a crucial factor in the outcome, besides reducing the match to thirty minutes each half. When play began, England started well. The reporter for the Advertizer, writing in the issue of January 22nd, noted that "Wales won the toss and elected to defend the goal nearest the gasometer", and defend they did, as they appear to have been put under severe pressure throughout the first half by England's forwards. England established a 2-0 lead after twenty minutes' play and maintained this score into the second half. The language of football reporting of the 19th century seems strange to modern eyes, England's goals being described in the following terms: "the English . . . were for a time kept at bay, but at last their efforts were crowned with success. A struggle took place on the left side of the Welsh goal, Bailey then middled the ball to Whitfield who passed it between the goals", thus 1-0, and for the second goal "a well-combined rush on the part of Mosforth and Whitfield ran the ball up to the visitors' goal. The latter then kicked it to Sorby, who scored the second goal to the credit of the English". Times change!

However, after half-time the Welsh were not to be denied, and they put their game together much better "passing the ball to each other in a very able manner", until ". . . at last Davies, Roberts and Price took the ball down the left side of the ground, Roberts cleverly centred it, and Davies kicked it under the tape, thus gaining a goal for Wales", making the score 2-1 for England. This is how the game ended, in victory for the English. The Welsh players were, however, far from disgraced, and indeed felt they had good cause for grievance. Shone had bad luck, his shot hitting the English post almost on full-time; but before this, Wales had even less fortune, as the foul weather played tricks on the players of both sides, reducing visibility to a few yards, and depriving Wales of a "good goal". In the words of the Advertizer "just before play ceased Davies claimed a foul against one of the opposing forwards. This being allowed, the ball should have been brought back to where the infringement of the law took place. As only those close to the spot were aware of the circumstances, the game continued, and after Roberts had sent the ball between the posts, the Welshmen, who thought matters were now level, were rather surprised that their efforts had been thrown way and that the goal could not be reckoned".

The Advertizer did not fail to draw conclusions from the result, claiming it to have been "virtually a tie", and pointing out validly that Wales had been reduced to ten men for much of the match, Heywood having been hurt early on. Oswestry were due to take on their rivals Wrexham the following Saturday in the third round of the Welsh Cup, and according to the 'Tizer, the result was a foregone conclusion: "the result of Saturday's play goes far to raise the hopes of the success of the Oswestry team for the Welsh Cup, as if with the assistance of two players they could make such a show against the pick of England, they should have little difficulty in disposing of their local rivals". A logical conclusion, one might think, but football seldom works out logically—Oswestry went to Wrexham, and, possibly through over-confidence, lost 2-0. Once more, the tie was played in treacherous conditions, which forced the match to be switched from an ice-covered Wrexham Racecourse. Wrexham supporters felt vindicated, and showered the Advertizer with criticism of the Welsh committee for its selection for January 18th.

Further Reading

Books on Oswestry

Cathrall, William   The History of Oswestry, etc.
Oswestry: George Lewis, 1855 (reprinted Shropshire Libraries 1973)

Leighton, Stanley   Records of the Corporation of Oswestry *in* Transactions of the Shropshire Archaeological and Natural History Society vols 2-6.
Shrewsbury: Shropshire Archaeological Society, 1879-1883.

Oakley, Richard R.   A history of Oswestry School
London: Seeley Service & Co., 1965

Oswestry parish registers
1558-1949: Shropshire Record Office
1950 to date: St. Oswald's Church, Oswestry

Owen, Thomas   Personal reminiscences of Oswestry fifty years ago
Oswestry: Thomas Owen & Sons, 1904

Parry-Jones, J.   The story of Oswestry Castle
Shrewsbury: Shropshire Archaeological Society, 1893

Pratt, Derrick   Oswestry town wall
Oswestry: Border Counties Archaeological Group, 1981

Price, William   History of Oswestry from the earliest period
Oswestry : William Price, 1815

Roberts, Askew   Contributions to Oswestry history
Oswestry: Woodall & Venables, 1881

Roberts, Brynley F.   Edward Lhuyd, the making of a scientist (G. J. Williams Memorial Lecture)
Cardiff: University of Wales Press, 1980

Slack, W. J. (ed)   The Lordship of Oswestry, 1393-1607
Shrewsbury: Wilding & Son (for Shropshire Archaeological Society), 1951

Smith, Llinos B.   Oswestry *in* Boroughs of mediaeval Wales, edited by Ralph A. Griffiths, pp 218-242
Cardiff: University of Wales Press (for the History & Law Committee of the Board for Celtic Studies), 1978

Watkin, Isaac   Oswestry, with an account of its old houses, shops, etc.
London: Simpkin, Marshall, Hamilton, Kent & Co.
Oswestry: Thomas Owen & Son, 1920 (reprinted Newgate Books, Oswestry 1982)

General Works

Camden, William — Britannia (English translation)
London: A. Swalle, 1695

Campbell, J. L. & Thomson, Derick — Edward Lhuyd in the Scottish Highlands, 1699-1700
Oxford: Clarendon Press, 1963

Charles, B. G. — The Welsh, their language and place names in Archenfield and Oswestry *in* Angles and Britons, (O'Donnell Lectures) pp 85-110.
Cardiff: University of Wales Press, 1967

Christiansen, Rex & Miller, Robert William — The Cambrian Railways
    Vol. 1 1852-1888
    Vol. 2 1889-1968
    Newton Abbot: David & Charles
    Vol. 1, 2nd ed. 1971
    Vol. 2 1968

Dictionary of Welsh biography down to 1940
Oxford: Blackwell, 1959

Eyton, Robert William — Antiquities of Shropshire
London: J. R. Smith, 1854-60

Gasquoine, C. P. — The story of the Cambrian
Oswestry: Woodall, Minshall, Thomas & Co., 1922

Jenkins, J. Geraint — The Welsh woollen industry
Cardiff: National Museum of Wales (Welsh Folk Museum), 1969·

Kidner, Roger Wakely — The Cambrian Railways
Tanglewood, South Godstone: Oakwood Press, 1954

Leland, John — Itinerary of John Leland in or about the years 1535-1543
Vol. 3 edited by Lucy Toulmin Smith
London: Centaur Press, 1964

Mendenhall, T. C. — The Shrewsbury drapers and the Welsh wool trade in the XVI and XVII centuries
Oxford: Oxford University Press
London: Geoffrey Cumberlege, 1953

Rowley, Trevor — The Shropshire landscape
London: Hodder & Stoughton, 1972

Thomas, R. D. — Industries of the Morda Valley
Oswestry: Woodall, Minshall, Thomas & Co., 1939
(reprinted Shropshire Libraries 1978)

Tudor Economic Documents
          Vol. 1 Agriculture and industry, edited by R. H. Tawney and E. Power
          London: Longmans, Green, 1924

Victoria County History
          Shropshire vols. I, II, III, VIII
          Oxford: Oxford University Press (for the University of London Institute of Historical Research), 1908-1979

Wilson, E. A.
          The Ellesmere and Llangollen canal
          Chichester: Phillimore, 1975

Wren, Wilfred J.
          The Tanat valley
          Newton Abbot: David & Charles, 1968

Newspapers and periodicals
Border Counties Advertizer (1849 to date)
Bye-Gones relating to Wales and the Border Counties (1871-1939)
Shrewsbury Chronicle (1772 to date)
    (especially for its first 70 years)
Shropshire Star (1964 to date)

Other Useful Sources
Transactions of the Caradoc & Severn Valley Field Club
Country Quest
Y Cymmrodor: Transactions of the Cymmrodorion Society of London
Eddowes Shrewsbury Journal (1843-1891)
Transactions of the Shropshire Archaeological & Natural History Society
Shropshire Magazine